"Joan Morgan schools like no other. While reading this masterful, rich, and amazingly concise cultural history of the "Nina Simone defecating on your microphone" Nineties, I learned two lessons. One, you cannot tell the story of hip hop or Black womanhood in the 1990s without a deep understanding of the prototype for Black Girl Genius that is Lauryn Hill. And two, you cannot tell the story of hip hop or Black womanhood in the 1990s without the fiya-spitting, Jamaican, Bronx-girl pen of Joan Morgan. Lauryn gave us the soundtrack, the artistry, and the permission. Joan and her crew of badass, pioneering hip-hop journalists, many of whom are featured here, continue to give us the language and the frameworks to understand the singularity of turn-of-the-twenty-first-century Black cultural production. Absent either of these Black girl geniuses, the story is incomplete. Indeed, she begat this."

—**BRITTNEY COOPER,** author of *Eloquent Rage:
A Black Feminist Discovers Her Superpower*

"Pioneer hip-hop feminist Joan Morgan takes on Lauryn Hill, the complicated star whose monumental album changed the world, and we finally get the loving, vibrant, critical attention the artist, her work, and her generation has been due. This book is a listening companion with attitude and a sureshot conversation starter. You may never hear Ms. Hill the same again."

—**JEFF CHANG,** author of *We Gon' Be Alright:
Notes on Race and Resegregation*

"The dope shit always needs a remix, if only to be reminded of the brilliance of the original joint. And if you were on the scene back in '98, you knew it would be Joan Morgan who would remix *The Miseducation of Lauryn Hill*, because who else would it be but a Caribbean sister stepping in the world fly AF and with the gift of verse? Lauryn might have *Begat This*, but Joan Morgan is giving it back to us all lovely and new and as vital as it was that summer of '98."

—**MARK ANTHONY NEAL,** Chair of the Department of
African & African American Studies at Duke University

"With *She Begat This*, Joan Morgan brings the full lyrical prowess of her unstoppable flow and ferocious prose to tell the multilayered saga of Lauryn Hill's seminal masterpiece. Morgan serves up an intimate artistic portrait that is compassionate, unflinching, and imbued with the razor-sharp analysis and from-the-heart truth telling that made her a legend of hip-hop journalism."

—**DANIEL JOSÉ OLDER,** *New York Times* bestselling author
of *Shadowshaper* and *Dactyl Hill Squad*, winner of
the International Latino Book Award

"A new book by Joan Morgan would be cause for celebration whether it was about Lauryn Hill, Bunker Hill, or ant hills. But for hip hop's founding feminist and most incisive critic to apply the force of her intellect, the power of her memory, and the dexterity of her cultural mixology to a record so fraught with meaning and misunderstanding makes me feel the way I did the first time I heard the needle drop on 'Lost Ones.' In fact, I'm dancing with one fist in the air as I write this."

—**ADAM MANSBACH,** #1 *New York Times* bestselling author

"Part storytelling, part cultural commentary; part cipher, part praise-song, Joan Morgan's *She Begat This* is perhaps the most necessary read for the present Black cultural moment. Twenty years after the release of Lauryn Hill's *The Miseducation of Lauryn Hill*, Morgan's frame of the moment solidifies its importance as hip-hop zeitgeist occurrence—as catalyst to our age of fierce Black outrage and millennial Black claim. That it also serves to re-establish Morgan as hip-hop feminism's high priest must be recognized, and we mean it in the manner of hip-hop imperative . . . *Recognize!*"

—**ROGER BONAIR-AGARD,** National Book Award nominee
and author of *Bury My Clothes* and *Where Brooklyn At?*

She Begat This

20 YEARS OF *THE MISEDUCATION OF LAURYN HILL*

Joan Morgan

Acclaimed author of
When Chickenheads Come Home to Roost

37INK

—

ATRIA

NEW YORK LONDON TORONTO SYDNEY NEW DELHI

37 INK
ATRIA

An Imprint of Simon & Schuster, Inc.
1230 Avenue of the Americas
New York, NY 10020

First 37 Ink/Atria Books hardcover edition August 2018

37 INK / ATRIA B O O K S and colophon are trademarks of Simon & Schuster, Inc.

For information about special discounts for bulk purchases, please contact Simon & Schuster Special Sales at 1-866-506-1949 or business@simonandschuster.com.

The Simon & Schuster Speakers Bureau can bring authors to your live event. For more information or to book an event, contact the Simon & Schuster Speakers Bureau at 1-866-248-3049 or visit our website at www.simonspeakers.com.

Interior design by Silverglass
Jacket design by Albert Tang & David Wu
Jacket art © BBBar/DepositPhotos; © themacx/iStock/Getty Images Plus

Manufactured in the United States of America

10 9 8 7 6 5 4 3 2 1

Library of Congress Cataloging-in-Publication Data has been applied for.

ISBN 978-1-5011-9525-9
ISBN 978-1-5011-9527-3 (ebook)

THIS BOOK IS DEDICATED TO MY SON, SULE MURRAY,
WHO IS ALWAYS THE REASON AND OFTEN THE INNOVATION.
I AM #FOREVERTEAMUS.

Contents

Foreword

2018

"I invented millennials" is something I've been known to say on occasion. I say it because it's actual, factual, and, I think, funny— if not a tad bit juvenile. But the younger people I sometimes feel compelled to say this to don't find as much humor in the snark. I'm still chuckling. My bad.

Let me clarify. By "I," I mean "we." And by "we," I mean the black women of the hip-hop generation. The once twenty- and early thirtysomethings, who, like me were both shaped by hip-hop culture and did the shaping—from the margins and the popping-ass center. Consequently, we set a new world order in motion. When I say we invented millennials, it's not because a new generation of black women and men aren't incredibly dope unto themselves— inspiring even. It's because we were the first ones who, without much armor, reported live from the crossroads and through the cross fire of race, class, and gender during the explosion of a global multibillion-dollar industry. One that was built on our backs. Remember when you looked up and it seemed like black culture just became culture? For better or worse, that was our export. While our younger sisters in particular claimed much-needed language to navigate a post–hip-hop world (*hey, Kimberlé Crenshaw's theory of intersectionality, hey*) in the 1990s, we were the mavericks. We manifested the politics of a spanking-new Black feminism and told her she could bring alla her homies—contradiction, agency, image, desire, power, media, sex, white folks—to the hood and the academy. And we did all this while steeped in a cultural ecosystem that was developing at warp speed, fueled by the machinations of young men that were often toxic. Young men that we loved.

Pause.

(Thank you, Joan Morgan. Have I said this before? You're a hero. Before actually knowing you, your culture reporting made this hostile hip-hop world make sense for twenty-two-year-old black girl me. What were you, a full twenty-five? Your brave, early, sometimes girly, always womanly voice made it less crazy-making to be all the impossible things I was—which was in love with a problematic thing. In your work all those years ago, you saw both the magic in my red lipstick and my Timbs, and your ability to see that sparked everything. And by "my" I mean "our.")

Women of the hip-hop generation were the frontliners of what we now know to be Wakandan warriorship. It's an easy reference at the time of this writing, looking back to the future, but honestly, how can one resist making the comparison between this unique generation of women and the Dora Milaje—the battalion of fighter women in Marvel's 2018 film *Black Panther*? Purist hip-hop culture and its burgeoning conversation between young black America and the other America were T'Challa and Killmonger. But be clear. It was us girls who fought and saved the nation.

(And that is how we gave birth to millennials.)

1998

There was a late-summer day in 1998 when all hell broke loose. Everyone in the music industry and in the world of hip-hop journalism knew it was coming, something solo from Lauryn Hill, but how could we have known?

For context, the better of us had already conceded that Hill was the best emcee in the Fugees, the three-man/one-woman "New Jerus" rap group led by the impressive music man, Haitian-proud Wyclef Jean. With the exception of perhaps being a few too many things to Hill—leader and lover—if you were Wyclef at the time, the biggest problem with your artist was likely that she was great at a lot of shit. As deft and raw a singer as Hill was an emcee (and a compelling actor as well—do watch *Sister Act 2* on Netflix), over the years there was a distinct evolution of her artistry in the context of a group. Her star didn't just sit higher in the sky; it was brighter. When the Fugees dropped *The Score* in '96, the ante was all the way upped. The group was enjoying critical acclaim and the streets couldn't have loved them more. Clef and the crew took home the coveted Grammy for Best Rap Album that year, yet both musically and personally, it was becoming clearer that a black woman needed her space. The album's outlier moment belonged to Hill. Really, that was it: her exceptional cover of Roberta Flack's "Killing Me Softly" was the canary in the coal mine. It was Wyclef's production, but unbeknownst to him, it also the beginning of the Fugees's end. More than anything, the song solidified the feverish anticipation about what the unicorn might attempt on her own, and where she would take things if given the chance. She was just that bad, "bad" meaning "good," and the world was bursting at the seams with curiosity.

I can't assert that Hill was the first woman to ever say to the thing that confined her, "Who gon' stop me, Boo?" But in the space of time between 1996 and 1998, it sure felt like she was the first to say it.

Completely free of the band, the man, and their not-so-well-kept secrets, Hill quickly transformed from girl to woman. She fell in love with Rohan Marley (son of Bob) and became pregnant with her first child. She was self-actualizing before our eyes, essentially proving at just twenty-two years old that she was a black magic woman capable of anything at a time when few believed female artists—especially those in a hip-hop world—could do just any-thing and sell millions of records. Many of us murmured regres-sive, sexist thoughts. *How will she mother and rock crowds? And she was just about to blow up!* It was shameful. But on that August 1998 day when *The Miseducation of Lauryn Hill* finally hit airwaves? Oh my God.

Lucky for us, like everyone in their twenties, Hill imagined herself wiser than she really was. That egotistical sense of righ-teous natural-womanness and Hill's expanding spirituality colored the musical journey she took us on. It was everything and it com-pelled her to preach. Of course, we understood that her messages weren't always prescriptive. How could they be? She was messier than she ever owned—but they were always her truth. What Hill had traversed and triumphed in the two years before *Miseducation* all seemed to make its way to the studio. Every ounce of the album was soaked in the personal. Her broken heart and her missteps. Her fierceness and new no fucks to give. It was as if she knew what was wrong with men, women, the race, and hip hop too. *Ase.* It was one of those rare times that a black woman was speaking and the world had sense enough to listen.

If only we could calculate the place X time X impact equation of Beyoncé's 2016 album *Lemonade* and measure it against the place X time X impact of 1998's *Miseducation*. Perhaps then more cynical minds, those who missed it in real time, might fully grasp the gravity of the *Miseducation* moment. Above the fray, with a baby in tow, and in a single chess move, King Lauryn called "Check." And she did it minus the future technology, the kind that allows a present-day artist to personally control the timing and instrument of distribution. Lauryn Hill, a black woman straight outta hip hop, had disrupted everything. Immediately upon release, the album hit number one on the Billboard 200. Week one sales (more than 420,000 copies) broke the record for female artists of all genres. By 1999, *Miseducation* had ultimately represented many female firsts: eight times platinum, ten Grammy nominations and five wins, making it quite literally both the album of the year and the Album of the Year.

I did not say rap album.

1999

Perhaps because culture calls for witnesses, Joicelyn Dingle and I launched *Honey* magazine in that same year when *Miseducation* really took root. Billed as the first national magazine for the women of the hip-hop generation, it was a long time coming. Naturally, it was Hill's full head of jet-black locs that filled the frame of the publication's coveted preview issue. With her back against a honeycomb set, a Tiffany silver bee dangling from a necklace and her head tilted just so, Hill was photographed nibbling on her finger pensively. Frozen in time and with thoughts of her own, Hill was all of us. She was a perfect encapsulation of what we were as a new tribe of black women and girls pushing all kinds of boundaries: sweet, thick, pure, brown, sticky. The cover line simply read, "Taste the Future." As *Honey*'s first editor in chief, I take enormous pride in our prophetic lens. The future was about our seat at the table.

That preview issue wasn't sold on newsstands; it was an early promotional piece for "influencers," long before that's what they were called. By the launch of our first national newsstand issue in 1999, it fully felt as though a black-girl movement was afoot. It was a feeling affirmed by the rise of "hip-hop feminism" and the rise in "hip-hop journalism" and confirmed by the timely work of godmother proper to both, Joan Morgan. "The enormous task of saving our lives falls on nobody else's shoulders but ours," she wrote in *When Chickenheads Come Home to Roost: A Hip-Hop Feminist Breaks It Down*—then the spot-on curriculum for the Hip Hop Women's Studies 101 course Hill had already pre-registered us for. Now it's a seminal read for anyone who seeks to understand some of the bigger questions before our generation's feminist intellectuals. In that very first issue of *Honey*, prescient as we were, we interviewed Morgan, who said, "I really wanted a book and a title that wasn't about victimization or blame. I wanted to create a space where women feel comfortable, but also talk about the way that we are, if not responsible, then complicit in our situation. It's not just strong women versus weak women. It's a combination all the time."

If I am gushing here, allow me to acknowledge that it is a great privilege (and a moment that's full circle AF!) to be asked to write the introduction to another work by Joan Morgan, *She Begat This*, a book about what, twenty years later, is still arguably the greatest album of a generation—my generation—the work of a young black woman who rose to fame through hip hop and who also happened to grace the cover of my first big thing.

Note: What follows on these pages shouldn't be confused with a dissection of Lauryn Hill (the forty-three-year-old woman, mother of six, and grandmother of one) or of her assorted and sundry personal choices and life events in the many seasons since *Miseducation*. It is not that. Like me, Morgan has spent a good portion of the time since then nurturing and teaching and being nurtured by and learning from a new wave of black feminists. The process is often both a breaking down and a building up of today's powerful young women—women who are reminiscent of both the Lauryn Hills and the Joan Morgans I recall from my twenties. "Everything," I've been known to say to them, "in its place and time."

She Begat This is a reminder of place and time. It calls attention to the importance of the holistic context of the subjects from yesterday, the ones we want to parse apart and understand today. This is critical when your audience is prone to see through the lens of the Internet of things. *She Begat This* considers time and place and place and time while exploring the full 360 degrees of not only *The Miseducation of Lauryn Hill* but also the ideas and movements behind the masterpiece's cultural universe. This is essential, lest some younger, duly creative folk try to imagine a world where, say, being in a '90s generation of fly, black women with natural hair was the same as being in Generation #teamnatural.

Because it wasn't.

Miseducation arrived in a time before the hashtag. To be a caesar-cut-rocking Joan Morgan (as she was back then) or dread-locked L-Boogie, a hip-hop generation naturalista, was to be part of a glorious, unspoken sisterhood—one not popular enough yet to be affirmed by aisles upon aisles of products, hair-texture ranking systems, A-list black celebrities, white women's magazine covers, or the very men of hip hop that too many of us desired but who gave us very little attention. It was an intentional choice, often burdened mistakenly with assumptions about one's personal politics and with nowhere near enough freedom to be merely a hairstyle. Imagine. A path with no hashtag or phenomena to affirm what we collectively always knew but hadn't yet dared publicly call forth: We were both a trend and a dope-ass movement. But don't cry for us, Argentina. A generation later, that's been covered.

The point here is that the twentieth anniversary of *Miseducation* is a cause for celebration, for more reasons than may be immediately apparent. In addition to being worthy of recognition as the profound, historic musical moment it was, this anniversary, for a specific swath of black women in America, is a remembrance. For us, it is a harkening back to a complicated, truly iconic era when real-life personal timelines were pockmarked by sweeping cultural moments: booming, resounding, no-going-back, ready-or-not moments that seemingly created new possibilities overnight. For these black women, it is a recalling of not only what the release of *Miseducation* symbolized to the world, but also the myriad of beautiful notions it set off in ours. As such, it is my humble honor to connect for you the teeny-tiny dots between the #BlackGirlMagic prequel era, if you will, and the contemporary critical thinking of a certain hip-hop feminist about Lauryn Hill's first and only full studio album two decades ago. That connection matters. And Morgan, by including the lengthy reflections of women whose cultural critiques and creative contributions have helped define and articulate the '90s or interpret it today—writers and editors Raquel Cepeda, Joicelyn Dingle, Karen Good Marable, dream hampton, Akiba Solomon, deejays Belinda Becker and Lynnée Denise, image activists Dr. Yaba Blay and Michaela Angela Davis, movement makers Beverly Bond and Tarana Burke, reggae superstar Nadine Sutherland and hip-hop feminist Dr. Treva B. Lindsey to name a few—has given us more than a celebration of an auspicious musical anniversary. *She Begat This* is a reflection point for two intersecting generations of black women.

Because even if the worldwide fervor during *Miseducation*'s release missed you in real time, it isn't as though you don't know its very crevices. At some point, the urgency of Carlos Santana's guitar riff meeting Lauryn's pleas on "Ex-Factor" has probably taken you out, and the soulful beauty of D'Angelo on "Nothing Even Matters" has made you desperately yearn for something or someone you knew you shouldn't—at least once. You've probably done the imaginary (or real) dick grab when L-Boogie murders the very opening line on "Lost Ones." And no matter who we love today or what gender expression they are, we've all felt sorry enough for ourselves and have been summarily healed by listening to "I Used to Love Him" again and again.

Right?

Well, knowing and loving this extraordinarily special album is not the challenge, even after all this time. Finding widespread agreement that it belongs in the canon of "Classics of the People" along with joints like Stevie Wonder's *Hotter than July*, Marvin Gaye's *What's Going On,* Mary J. Blige's *My Life* or A Tribe Called Quest's *The Low End Theory* isn't so hard. To speak of the great musical resonance of this work, for the music critic, will be infinitely par for the course.

The challenge, here and now, is simple. Blast this entire masterful curation, all sixteen tracks, one lazy Sunday afternoon when the sun is piercing your windows so gloriously that cleaning almost feels like joy. Do that and . . . remember the time. It doesn't take firsthand memory to reverently consider the state of, the world of, the grace of black women and girls who were once on the cusp of a new millennium. All it takes is the music and will. With Morgan as our guide, this cool, critical book puts us, so sweetly, on a path toward knowing, really knowing, the brilliant, singular offering of *The Miseducation of Lauryn Hill*. Let's make it our portal to reflect on all that has and hasn't happened to black women and girls in the past twenty years.

—*Kierna Mayo, Long Island, New York, 2018*

1 / *Everything Is Everything*

L-Boogie's "Superstar" rises from behind the bar of Chez Lucienne and cuts across the din of the Lenox Avenue restaurant. It's a Tuesday night, which means the strip is poppin' and the spot is predictably filled with thirty- to seventysomethings, all sporting the particular mix of blackness so signature to Harlem. A quick scan reveals well-heeled professionals and government workers, sartorially inclined artists and wizened old hustlers, wide-eyed recent transplants and a seasoned old guard. The accents that pepper their revelry expose antecedents that span the global South. Mississippi to Mali. Accra to the Antilles. Brixton to Bed-Stuy. Still Harlem, despite the increasing number of white faces or the proliferation of new eateries boasting fussy fusion menus and downtown priced cocktails. In deference to this fact, the bartender assists the evening's transition from the cocktail to dinner hours with a predictable mix of '70s cookout classics, '80s R&B, and an amalgam of '90s soul and temperate hip hop. *The Miseducation of Lauryn Hill* is the apparent fave; all sixteen tracks woven diligently throughout. This is a realization I greet with an audible "Fuck."

That came out wrong. I loved *Miseducation*, at least as much as the nineteen million or so folks who've brought it since 1998. I'd even go as far as to say I probably loved it more than every mofo in those governing bodies that bestowed it with seventeen cumulative Billboard, American Music, Grammy, and MTV awards. Why? Because I was one of the score of hip-hop-loving and/or pregnant women who swore the album was soundtracking her life. And I still love it enough that when, almost twenty years later, a 2017 NPR roundup, "Turning the Tables: The 150 Greatest Albums Made by Women," ranked it number two, (Joni Mitchell's classic *Blue* was number one) I decided to give that decision a pass—although I'll leave it to the article's writers to defend how *Miseducation* managed to beat out Nina Simone's *I Put a Spell on You*, Aretha Franklin's *I Never Loved a Man the Way I Love You,* and Carole King's *Tapestry* since that's a claim I'm sure not even the woman currently known as Ms. Hill could reasonably stake.

My response was prompted by fatigue. Ever since I'd agreed to write a book on *Miseducation*'s twentieth anniversary, the album had been on heavy rotation. Tonight's dinner was supposed to be an escape. The goddaughter, thirty-two, and my dining partner for the evening, found the attempt to find respite here both amusing and naïve.

"Well, what did you expect?" she asked, referencing the amount of middle-aged folks in the crowd. "This is exactly her demographic."

"I mean, I get it," she continues. "I loved it too. When I was thirteen." The silent, but definitely implied, "Before I knew better," begs a follow-up question.

"And now?" I ask. "Do you still listen to it?" "No," she responds. "Not really. Nowhere near as much. I mean the whole thing is just so Hotep. She's so judge-y."

The admittedly froggy "Fuck you mean judge-y?" that instinctively runs through my head is a function of well-honed, former hip-hop journo reflexes, the kind of shit that'll always take place when someone critiques one of your top five. And when it comes to best emcee barometers, that holy trinity of lyrics, delivery, and flow—L-Boogie circa 1996–2002 was one of the best emcees of all time. Pause and note: I did not say one of the best female emcees. And I did not stutter. One of the best to ever do it and during the era routinely referred to as hip-hop's golden age. The bar was set mad high. To put her arrival in context, when *The Score*, the Fugees' critically acclaimed sophomore album, dropped in 1996, it joined a cohort of bangers that included Jay-Z's *Reasonable Doubt*, OutKast's *ATLiens*, Nas's *It Was Written*, Lil' Kim's *Hard Core* and Foxy Brown's *Ill Na Na*, which were all released in that same year. Punctuate that with the hand claps it deserves.

Commercially speaking, the genre had also worked through some of its growing pains. The '90s was the decade that hip hop broke through its previously gold ceiling to become a billion-dollar industry, hitting the dual sweet spots of artistic achievement with all the material trappings of platinum success. "We were definitely in this arrogant phase of weeding out the bullshit," says Schott Free, former senior vice president of A&R at LOUD Records and the executive producer of era greats like Mobb Deep, Dead Prez, and Roc Marciano. "At this point, if you put in the time, came up with a masterpiece, and packaged it right, you were going to get your just due. If you were making something worth hearing and that people loved, it was going to speak for itself."

By now, the framing of the Fugees' (comprised of Hill, Wyclef Jean, and Pras Michél) origin story as the greatest thing in hip hop that almost didn't happen is a well-known tale, but it is one worth recounting here since, at least according to Jayson Jackson's recollection, it was Hill's noteworthy talent on their otherwise meh debut (*Blunted on Reality*, 1994) that helped save the group from getting dropped. Jackson, one of the producers responsible for the Oscar-nominated documentary *What Happened, Miss Simone?*, was Hill's former manager and close friend. "At the time I was an intern at Columbia Records for a product manager. We had four groups," says Jackson. "The Fugees was one of them. I remember listening to *Blunted on Reality* and feeling like it was all over the place, but one particular song, "Some Seek Stardom," was a stand-out. It was just Lauryn. The shit that she was saying, the way she was rhyming and singing it, made me go, 'Yo. This girl is incredible.' Lauryn was still filming *Sister Act 2* at the time, but it was completely clear that as an artist, she was doing some new shit. She had a distinct voice. She was a star."

Of the four groups assigned to Jackson's boss, only one, the '90s girl group Xscape, was performing well enough to stay on the label. As Jackson watched the other two groups get unceremoniously dropped, he urged his boss to do something. "There was this Mega Banton song, 'Sound Boy Killing,' that was on the radio and [was] hot at the time. I was like, 'yo, get the motherfucka who did that.'" The "something" was a remix and the motherfucka in question was a Caribbean-American producer named Salaam Remi, whose trademark was a sonic ability to seamlessly cross the cultural hyphen to traffic dancehall vibes between urban sounds. In a Hot 97 interview, radio deejay Charlamagne Tha God playfully referred to Remi's production as "the green card for Jamaican artists." Remi, whose long roster includes Super Cat, Mega Banton, Patra, and later Amy Winehouse, Nas, and Fergie, sees it that way too. Referencing a moment in the '90s where dancehall and reggae enjoyed an unprecedented popularity in American music, Remi said, "It was all the stuff that was coming out of Jamaica that needed to get on the radio for hip hop and R&B. A lot of those songs were stuck at the airport, so to speak. I got them the visas that [helped] them get through."

Auspiciously for the Fugees, Remi agreed to do the remix for the relatively modest price of five grand, but it was money that they didn't have. In a display of typical hip-hop ingenuity, Jackson hustled the PR budget and said they were throwing a party. Instead, they used the money to pay Remi, who dug deep into the old-school hip-hop crates, sampled Harlem Underground's "Smokin Cheeba Cheeba" and flipped a lukewarm "Nappy Heads" into a fiyah bun remix. "They sent me the Fugees because they were Haitian, and they needed that bridge to figure out how to get this group into the mainstream," said Remi. "They had talent. They just hadn't figured out how to channel it. We were coming out of a moment in hip hop where groups like Onyx, who rhymed really fast, had a lot of success," Jackson explained. "But there was a shift going on. Hip hop was slowing down a bit more and Salaam knew it. He told the Fugees to slow their shit down, let people understand what they were saying, and add a catchy hook. Then he just bodied it."

The remix set the groundwork for the success of *The Score*. Journalist and dancehall expert Rob Kenner recalls a recent conversation with Wyclef regarding the concept behind the album. "Wyclef said they wanted to make a sound system project. The first draft of the award-winning cover of "Killing Me Softly" was originally conceived as "Killing a Sound Boy," said Kenner. A sound boy clash, for the uninitiated, is the Jamaican concept of battling deejays and the musical antecedent for deejay battles in hip hop. "If you go to a dance in Jamaica," explains Kenner, "they'll play anything from Peabo Bryson to Celine Dion to 'Tainted Love.'" It can be the corniest, poppiest record and they'll make it dancehall just by the way they present it. With *The Score* Wyclef was very explicitly taking up the Fugees as a sound system and incorporating the very Jamaican idea that "Any record that we pull out of the box can be dancehall-ified once we put our flavor and attitude on it." Despite its success, it was never meant to be a pop crossover record. It was very much conceived to be a "soundbwoy fi dead" record." That moment had been a long time coming, one that began with an ease in US immigration policies in the late 1960s that led to a dramatic increase in immigrants from the Caribbean, a significant number of which congregated in the ghettos of the Bronx and Brooklyn.

For reggae superstar Nadine Sutherland the Fugees embodied the paradigm of Caribbean people who live in America who embraced the duality of their culture. "The Fugees embodied the Caribbean experience in the diaspora," explained Sutherland. "I know that Lauryn Hill is American, but she's part of that movement and people identify her with that dual paradigm, that syncretic merging of the two cultures. It was the Fugees who helped me realize that Caribbean people living in the US could be like "Yeah, I'm

Caribbean. I love my country and I love my reggae, but I am also into hip hop and there was no major shift in their psyche to say it. They didn't feel as if they had to embrace one identity over the other. They were okay identifying with both." The introduction of cable television to Jamaica also gave Jamaicans on-island a new cross-cultural fluidity. "When BET came to Jamaica, we got access to everything that was happening in America. You could see people switch between cultures at the drop of a hat. Now it was nothing to see a Caribbean kid dancing to rap music and then turn around and dance to dancehall. It was an interesting paradigm."

Certified six times platinum in domestic sales alone, *The Score* made the Fugees one of the bestselling hip-hop groups in history, an accomplishment many attributed to the distinctiveness of the band's femmecee. There was no question that Lauryn Hill had heads on notice. Her award-winning cover of "Killing Me Softly" proved her mettle as a vocalist to contend with—and her valor. In the words of my girl Kierna Mayo, "No one is supposed to be able to touch Roberta Flack and survive." Lauryn did and subsequently hand-delivered the soul legend, wrapped anew, for an entirely new generation. When asked about her ability to flex deftly between emcee and songstress, Schott Free sums it up bluntly: "If Mary [J. Blige] is the queen of hip-hop soul, I don't know what we can call Lauryn, because Lauryn can actually rhyme. Mary can't rap. So, what do we call Lauryn? The influence?"

Even more significant for Free was the fact that it was accepted that Lauryn was writing all her own lyrics—at a time when the same could not be said of the two most popular female emcees. "People said that Jay-Z was writing a lot of Foxy [Brown's] stuff. If you go back now and listen to the flow you can hear it. And we already know the deal with Kim because I was right there watching Biggie do it. I've never heard anybody say, 'Oh I wrote Lauryn's rhymes.'" In the current era of feminist critique where women—in both scholarship and shit-talking—recast Lil' Kim as the transgressive architect of a new liberated sexuality in hip hop, Free's point is worth underscoring. That Kim could spit was never in question, but Free is not the only one convinced that at least some of the bars allegedly freeing the proverbial "P" were scripted by the same genius force that bought us "Dreams of Fucking an R-n-B Bitch." A fact worth putting in your feminist theory and fucking with. Along with the fact that Hill wrote her own rhymes and she wrote for and with her crew in an egalitarian, mixed-gendered, collaborative approach that was rare for hip hop at the time. By the time she dropped the "Ready or Not" verse that infamously invokes Elliot Ness, sess, witches brew, voodoo, and hexes then likens herself to Nina Simone right before firing the scatological shot heard around the world, it was Wu-Tang clear: Lauryn Hill was nothing to fuck with.

This was in part due to the utter uniqueness of Hill's components. Black. Female. Ivy Leaguer. A Columbia University English major blessed with a broad literary arsenal that simultaneously reflected her dexterity as a wordsmith and her acute understanding of the latent but deadly power in the economy of words. Lauryn was nice with hers. She had rhyme schemes that could stalk a lyrical adversary with panther-like precision. With a singsong playfulness, she could engage her silky alto and disarm anyone who made the mistake of taking her too lightly, then spit a death blow with the percussiveness of machine-gun rounds or metronomic machete swings, depending on her mood.

The Score's success placed the Fugees in league with The Roots—the biggest live hip-hop act at the time—comparisons were inevitable. Jackson saw it as apples and oranges. "With The Roots, people really weren't stressing their beats so much. It was more about their live instrumentation and the fact that these niggas, Black Thought and Malik B., could rhyme for hours. The Fugees," he continues, "were the poor man's Roots. Clef had the guitar. Jerry Duplessis was on the bass. Sometimes they had a drummer and a deejay. Sometimes just a deejay." Unlike The Roots, who were considered masters of live performance, the early Fugees shows were a mess, peppered with "cultural" acts of randomness meant to illustrate the group's ties and affinity to the Caribbean, and Haiti in particular. "Sometimes they'd bring a goat out on stage to give props to their Haitian roots. It was weird shit. The audience would laugh at them every time. People thought they were a joke." The laughter, however, would quickly end as soon as the crowds heard

Hill crooning from backstage, a strategy that the group quickly implemented. "Clef and Pras would come out rhyming and people would still be drinking and talking like, 'Whatever. These niggas is whack.' Then Lauryn would start singing from behind stage and the audience would go quiet, every fucking time. That's when it would be like, 'Okay. Now let's start the show.'"

The demand for Lauryn to go solo would start almost immediately, but Jackson, who watched the group's collaboration process almost from the beginning, felt assertions that Lauryn was carrying them with her talent were at best short-sighted. "I think the idea that her talent was being pimped to make a name for Clef and Pras began with the live shows. Then the press would write reviews of songs and claim Clef was a musical genius, which he is—that nigga can play every instrument, sing in four or five different languages—but then they'd start to write things that made it seem like Lauryn was just an instrument to his genius. Really, they were more like The Beatles. Clef was Paul and Lauryn was John. They were best together, but apart, they were some motherfuckers too." Time would bear this out. Wyclef Jean's first solo effort, *The Carnival*, was released in 1997 to wide critical acclaim and eventually certified at double platinum with two Grammy nominations. *Miseducation* followed it with ten nominations and a record-setting five wins, breaking the one set for female artists by Carole King and her album *Tapestry* in 1971.

There is more of course. The kind of things that become clearer after two decades of hindsight. For example, as critics we made much ado about the fact that *Miseducation* weaves a tapestry of sound that borrows liberally from soul, reggae, and hip hop but what is really more remarkable is that Lauryn was able to do that because she envisioned an identity for herself that was rooted in a diasporic blackness that seemed to not only travel seamlessly between Ethiopia, Newark, Brooklyn, Brixton, and Kingston but also through decades, pulling from black musical traditions of the 1960s, '70s, and '80s at will. Much of this has been shallowly attributed to her time in the Fugees and later her common-law marriage to Rohan Marley. But while her bandmates, Wyclef Jean and Pras Michél, bear the hyphenated negotiations of identity common to first- and second-generation immigrants, Lauryn Hill is strictly African American. There was no ackee and saltfish and boiled dumpling cooking in the Sunday morning kitchen of her childhood. No parents rousing her out of sleep with sharply punctuated patois. Instead, she deliberately wrote herself into the discourse of diaspora, drew on the global nature of black music, and fashioned herself a citizen of the world. She took from that legacy what she wanted and asked no one's permission, in part because she treated hip hop itself for what it is—a Caribbean-American art form. Understanding its roots, L-Boogie explored its routes. As a result, her blackness, and its reach, was ubiquitous.

She was also arresting. And not just because she arrived as a working actress (she had a reoccurring role on the soap *As the World Turns* and a lead in *Sister Act 2* under her belt), one who understood presence and how to werrrk a camera and command a stage. To quote writer, activist, and filmmaker dream hampton, "Lauryn Hill was our most beautiful pop star from that era. Line up Whitney, Janet, and Mariah. Lauryn was the most beautiful. Those wedges. Those legs. Those thigh-high shorts. She was just this perfect little thing." But while beautiful pop stars are the stuff of cliché, it was the type of beauty Lauryn Hill possessed that made her as much of a visual intervention as she was a musical one. Deep chocolate brown skin with a mane of dreadlocks, she was the type of post–fly girl pretty common to pre-gentrified Fort Greene and Bed-Stuy, but was completely ignored by the mainstream media. And if we are to be nakedly honest—and really, after twenty years in, why not?—by plenty of hip-hop era black men in ways that were demonstrated by both their dating and video casting choices. In a sea of sew-ins and relaxers, Lauryn was a naturalista long before YouTube tutorials talked black women through the radical choice of actually liking and growing our hair the way nature and our gene pool intended. And way before the twenty-first century's natural hair revolution created a half-billion-dollar industry of conveniences to support that choice.

Lithe and leggy, Lauryn was a fashionista deeply invested in a personal style, who liked nice things but seemed to flow above the fray of ghetto fabulousness and its accompanying tendency to serve as high-end designers' billboards. She liked her hip-hop tinged with a rootsy glam and hints of an ethereal '70s sexy grounded with sobering touches of militancy—a combo that was deceptively accessible, simultaneously aspirational, and ultimately inimitable. Making cover-girl moves where no dreadlocked black girl had gone before— *Harper's Bazaar, Cosmopolitan.* Shit. *Essence*—we have Lauryn Hill to thank for the present-day Gucci models who sport TWAs (teeny-tiny afros) and Saint Laurent girls showcasing blackety-black-black cornrows, the kind without extensions. In short, Lauryn was the visual precursor for #BlackGirlMagic and #BlackGirlsRock. We turned to her for soul affirmations that we were more than enough before the digital revolution granted us hashtags that enabled us to harness archives of similar fierceness easily on Instagram and Tumblr.

Routinely lauded for its themes of self-love, empowerment, and broken-heart-bounce-backs, *The Miseducation of Lauryn Hill* has earned itself the rank of classic in contemporary American popular culture. And yet, two decades after its debut in 1998, so little has been written about where and when *Miseducation* entered. More specifically, that it was sired by a '90s kind of girl at the end of a century that would dismantle the Berlin Wall, witness an act of American-on-Americans terrorism in Oklahoma, and usher in a digital age that would change the dynamics of human interaction and intimacy as we formerly knew it.

And because she was a '90s kind of black girl, she came into adulthood watching the police receive passes for brutalizing black bodies—the murders of Amadou Diallo and Eleanor Bumpurs and the beating of Rodney King—in ways the next century would render routine enough to warrant a #BlackLivesMatter movement. She saw a million black men march on Washington and watched Los Angeles burst into riotous flames. She also saw a lone black woman stand firm against the nomination of a black Supreme Court judge and far too many black people dismiss her claims of sexual harassment as a Jezebel's coercion with white racism. Specifically, as a black woman she would watch the white president who was jokingly (and ultimately ironically) referred to as the first black one, sign in legislature—the Violent Crime Control and Law Enforcement Act and the Personal Responsibility and Work Opportunity Reconciliation Act—that would devastate her community both politically and economically, systematically destabilizing the structural conditions necessary for #BlackLove to thrive for decades to come. She also saw a president whose own love triangle played itself out in a public scandal of an impeachment trial while the pain of her private one gifted a generation with its own vehicle for healing and catharsis.

And make no mistake about it. If you were a hip-hop-loving black girl in the '90s you were deeply in need of some healing. You'd already started steeling yourself for the battle ahead when hip hop, in its quest for commercial dominance, chose corporatization as its bedmate. By the time it was revealed to the world that virulent misogyny (not to mention homophobia) were going to be mainstay ingredients in its increasingly formulaic recipe for SoundScan success, you'd already peeped the writing on the wall. You, the black and brown women who'd helped create the hottest party of the late twentieth century were being summarily written off the guest list, while Becky and Barry Middle America were greeted at the velvet rope with VIP wristbands.

The music you loved rebranded you the sacrificial cow and left you to a careless death—one by thousands of lyrical lacerations. You were not alone. The '90s was the era when what was formerly "black" got rebranded as "urban." In turn, it opened up shop and rolled out a welcome mat and passed out flyers with hooker-level solicitations: "We sell culture here! Feel free to appropriate!" Meanwhile entire black music departments disappeared at record labels, absorbed and neutralized under the auspices of "pop." By the time Biggie and Pac were gunned down six days apart (1996 was a mixed bag like a mothafucka), you could hardly keep track of what you were crying for. We were still trying to create the language—for what it meant to love hip hop, black men, and still hold on to yourself.

But back to the judge-y goddaughter.

I'm feeling a bit defensive. After all, judge-y is the lack of grace millennials fail to grant the generation prior who didn't grow up with "binaries are bad!" and "gender is fluid!" as givens. The one that came of age before postblackness was a thing and PhDs in queer and hip-hop studies were possible. These were theories we had to learn, sometimes in the midst of creating them. I mean this literally. In 1998, I was home finishing the final edits on the book that would birth hip-hop feminism. And yes, I was listening to Lauryn.

Looking back, we were already barreling toward the shades of gray that millennials and the iGeneration see their world in. The shift from black and white was unsettling, full of conflicts and even more contradictions. For example, '90s blackness still had deep investments in respectability politics and often found itself in conflict with hip hop's penchant for valorizing the hood. At the same time, they were middle- and upper-class kids and rappers claiming ghetto authenticity, even if they had to lie about it. Journalist Akiba Solomon, who had just started her job as an assistant editor at *The Source* magazine when *Miseducation* dropped, recalls Lauryn being one of the few middle-class rappers who was actually honest about it. "Remember that line in 'That Thing,' 'Don't be a hard rock when you really are a gem'? It was one of my favorites,'" said Solomon. "Nowadays people would dismiss that as 'She's being a Hotep' and indulging in the politics of respectability or whatever, but back then it was really helpful for me to hear a woman say that—especially a woman like Lauryn who was undoubtedly from the culture and loved the culture but was making a commentary on girls 'acting hard.' It was the era of the gangsta bitch," Solomon explained, "and a lot of girls in hip hop identified with this hypermasculine idea of 'soldiering.' Kim and Foxy were the hot female rappers and they were rhyming about carrying drugs in your cooch on a Greyhound. Well, that was interesting imagery, but it didn't represent my experiences. Lauryn was a middle-class girl from suburban New Jersey who talked about class—working and middle—in her lyrics. For somebody like her to talk about the fullness of black experience was important and brave because at the time, there was a whole swath of people in hip hop pretending that they weren't middle class. Middle-class people were trying to hustle backward, and hood people were trying to appear wealthy. It was a weird and I would argue, self-destructive, take. Black people, and black women in particular, have multiple sides. Even the so-called hoodest of us also have middle-class concerns. Lauryn's lyric felt like air to me. The whole album did."

Similarly, the purists were obsessed with authenticity and called out the sellouts. The backpackers lamented they didn't see the same kinds of commercial success as the hard core.

And everybody wanted a magazine cover. In response, the decade seemed to organize itself by binaries and chose its camps accordingly. Everything seemed to be evaluated by markers of versus back then: East Coast vs. West Coast, positive vs. negative, gay vs. straight, hoes vs. queens. Even the Fugees's success was partially due to the ways they were positioned as the positive alternative to the violence that claimed Biggie and Pac's lives. Just like Lauryn's pedestal was partially built on a distinct fear and loathing for Kim and Foxy's hypersexuality. This was a practice that, to her credit, dream hampton knew we would ultimately have to undo. "I tried to get at it, even back then, in a review I wrote about Digable Planets," she laments. "I mean, what made us think that the person who was listening to Arrested Development wasn't also the same person who was listening to Ice Cube?"

I feel myself cutting the goddaughter some slack. The twenty years between us is the critical difference between the generation that grew up with hip hop as a given and the one that watched it move from subculture to center. And it wasn't just the music. With a hustler's spirit inscribed deep within its DNA, hip hop made new lanes and created new career possibilities. In turn, we got real carpe diem with our shit, dubbed ourselves the culture's keepers, and became its deejays, producers, music executives, writers, editors, publishers, entrepreneurs, directors, stylists, and designers. We were arrogant, opinionated, and indebted because hip hop changed our lives. I'm sure this made us judge-y as shit.

Besides, anyone who's ever listened to "Doo Wop (That Thing)" knows that Lauryn could be judge-y. Wrapped within the sweetness of its Motown-inspired melodies lies a lyrical smackdown of certain black girl aesthetics that heads are still in their feelings about. "Yup," laughs deejay Lynnée Denise, who admits to being "one of those gay women who was in love with her. That deep raspy voice and the way she would flip her looks between masculine hip-hop gear and then something really femme made me feel like Lauryn was challenging gender binaries early. But then she hit me with that." It was a conservative position on "fakeness vs. authenticity" that Lynnée felt she couldn't afford. "I'm sure Lauryn grew up with black women in Jersey who shaped her fashion sense—women who were wearing fake nails and weaves. Besides, she had fake locs."

(*Wait. What?*)

Lyrically she is guilty as charged, but the video for "Doo Wop (That Thing)" reveals a trickster's play, and the didactic morphs into a delicious dualism. "It's interesting to revisit it twenty years later," says Lynnée. "The split screen has new meaning. I associate it with her being a Gemini and her natural understanding of the power of dualism. Lauryn as rapper/singer, artist/scholar. There's a darkness to it that speaks afro-futurism, a kind of time travel and speculative re-telling of black folk's history in New York City in the last century. All the elements of us are there. She catches the spirit of NYC summer community gatherings. She's gesturing toward Brooklyn, home of the block party, or maybe NYC black life as a whole."

There's the obvious dualism of the two time periods, of course, the '90s vs. the '60s. It's a split screen but the two eras aren't equally weighted. Its aesthetic has more in common with 1970s cinematography—gritty with muted colors that still manage to pay acute attention to the range of tonality and texture in black skin—much more akin to old-school black and white than '90s music-video cinematography. It was the height of ghetto fabulousness, in a time when hip hop was invested in the cache of being able to show the world that blackness could move seamlessly in and out of multiple worlds—from the Hamptons to the hood—and using shinier, big budget optics to do it. The visual choices in "Doo Wop (That Thing)" (much more cinematographer Bradford Young than director Hype Williams) however, seem to be a subtle rejection of that. Even the sartorial choices it makes for the '60s—brothers are dressed in sharp, clean suits and brims (*hey, Mos Def, hey*) and the women are in Jackie O tea-length, A-line dresses—is a veneration of the past that even the present seems captured by.

And then here comes Lauryn, slaying in double time and flipping her own respectability politics on its head. On the right side of the screen she's that L-Boogie effortless sexy that became her trademark: wedge-heeled platforms, thigh-high miniskirt with a matching spaghetti-strapped tee topped with an oversize denim shirt—one that she selectively shimmies out of to reveal gorgeous chocolate shoulders and accompanying décolleté. On the left side she's serving us '60s girl-group perfection in a zebra print swing coat and matching trapeze dress and—wait for it—a flawless swoop bang beehive. Simultaneously reserving the right to indict hair weaves and fake hair while wearing a straight wig. "She's a shape-shifter," Lynnée reminds me. "Much like the science fiction writer Octavia Butler's character Anyanwu, and she wears each shape masterfully well."

She's right. Dismissing Lauryn here as purely judge-y and hypocritical is too flat of a read. When Hill rhymed that she was only human she was advocating for her right to be complicated and beautifully contradictory—and ours too, whether she realized it or not. "It's like this," says Dr. Yaba Blay, scholar, image activist and creator of the popular web series #ProfessionalBlackGirl. "What made that video so powerful was her saying I can be both of these seemingly contradictory things and they're both real. I can criticize it and still rock it. The video also gives us these images of the beauty salon and the barbershop, which are traditionally safe spaces for us to have these kinds of conversations. Lauryn was moving us away from those harsh spaces of judgment and closer to where we are now, which is more 'I know it's a problem but that don't mean I don't like it. Can we talk about it?' It's very similar to the work you do in *Chickenheads*: when it [came] out the following year and you told us you needed 'a feminism that fucked with the grays.' It's that moment in the late '90s when [we] get that shift and we're being encouraged to see ourselves as dynamic, fluid human beings that are both/and, not either/or."

Both, Goddaughter. Judge-y and liberatory.

So many female artists now are just talking about competing with each other for dick and a lot of black female artists [in the] '90s were making albums that were essentially all about "I love myself so much." But not all of us needed that. Some of us needed someone who represented us in all our contradictions and pain and could put it in a well-mixed album that sounded good. Lauryn was that girl. Her image was just really relatable. A lot of women could relate to being nice—as in being on top of your game—being beautiful and being in love with the wrong man. She was inspiring because she was like, "I'm dope. You can be dope too . . . But I am doper than you." Obviously. Oh, Lauryn had a little stankness to her, but I feel like women—women of color and black women in particular—can relate to that.

—Akiba Solomon

2 / That Thing

Ask a black girl to recall her favorite Lauryn Hill memory from the '90s and at least one of them will probably recall a magazine—big, beautiful, and glossy. The end of the '90s was the print era's last stand. That's not to suggest that it was ever a neat divide, but in the predigital age the distinction between newspapers and magazines was this: Newspapers were what you turned to find out what was happening, but magazines were what you turned to figure out what *mattered*. Charged with the lofty duty of not only reporting but also interpreting culture, what a magazine chose to report not only rendered it visible, it also rendered it legible. Magazines had cultural capital.

If you were a black girl (and a writing or editing one at that), you waited anxiously to see if this was the month your favorite glossy would finally acknowledge your existence, all the while knowing that your appearances were exceedingly rare. If you were a black girl of the dark chocolate/dreadlocked/afroed/caesar-cut/hip-hop

gen/afro-bohemian/nose-ringed/ghetto-born/Ivy League–schooled/
Gucci-and-Timberland-loving variety, you already knew better
than to try to find yourself in *Essence*, let alone *Elle*. In the case
of the former (for which I wrote regularly), a frank, early convo
with an editor who wanted to see me succeed produced this bit
of wisdom: "Do yourself a favor," she said. "When you pitch story
ideas here, think of the Midwest and not of your five girlfriends
in New York who you meet for cappuccinos." Again, this is before the ubiquity of Starbucks, when coffee in New York was that
thing sold in Greek cups in bodegas and cost fifty cents, and
cappuccino-drinking black girls were so singularly rare MC Lyte
dropped a whole track extoling the drink's virtues in 1989.

The '90s was the decade that publishing, advertisers, and the
film industry hadn't been entirely disabused of the lie that black faces
and stories could not sell to mainstream (read white) consumers. An
example? *Essence*, the leading black women's magazine in the nation couldn't get the same fashion advertising as *Vogue*—despite the
fact that both had a subscriber base that exceeded 1 million and re-
search consistently demonstrated that black people's combined buy-
ing power was an estimated half trillion. (It currently hovers at 1.3
trillion). Even when presented with these numbers, they countered
by saying that black women weren't their desired consumers.

Hip hop went on to disprove that when fashion houses discovered that Gucci on a rapper could transform its entire accessories

market base, and Terry McMillan's *Waiting to Exhale* proved publishers' long-standing argument that blacks didn't read was false as hell—a revelation that gave birth to new genres like urban romance and hip-hop lit. It also paved the way for a new wave of black filmmakers including Spike Lee, John Singleton, and the Hughes and Hudlin brothers. Even with numerous successes, it was a battle that had to be fought time and again. Why do you think we organize and ride so hard for black filmmakers we want to see win on opening night? (*Hey, Ava DuVernay, hey*) Hopefully *Black Panther*'s success as, at least at the time of this printing, one of the highest-grossing superhero movies of all time will kill that convo once and for all.

So it meant something that by the end of the '90s, Lauryn Hill was not only on the cover of countless magazines, she was on covers that *mattered*. In 1999, when *Time* put Lauryn Hill on its February 8 cover, it had placed only seventeen black figures on its covers throughout the '90s—out of a total of 525 issues. Only five—including Bill Cosby, Bill T. Jones, Toni Morrison, and Oprah Winfrey—worked in arts and entertainment. Lauryn Hill was the only musician. (See "Deconstructing: Lauryn Hill's Rise and Fall, 15 Years After *The Miseducation of Lauryn Hill*," Max Blau, *Stereogum*, August 23, 2013).

Akiba Solomon has a story she loves to tell: "When I first started out in magazines, I was at *Jane*. I remember going to my editors and saying, 'I think we really need to do a feature on Lau-

ryn Hill.' They were like, 'That Fugee girl? No. What's the story?'
Then she came out on the cover of *Bazaar,* and I was like. 'Fuck
y'all.' I was so happy because *Bazaar* was considered high fashion,
dope and adult." The *Harper's Bazaar* double cover was a thing
of tremendous beauty, featuring a solo image of beaming Hill in
white slacks, red boots, and expertly flip-curled locs on one side
and a denim shorts, faux fur, and beret-wearing Hill surrounded
by gorgeous little black kids on the other. The cover was a radical
departure for the magazine, which, despite being led by the legendary and absolutely visionary editor in chief, the late Liz Tilberis, was categorically whiter than white.

"But it wasn't just that people outside the culture were starting
to see Lauryn," Solomon reiterates. "It was also how she showed
up. She went on that cover and she was still Lauryn. She was like
'Y'all come to me.' She was really the first black woman artist
that I'd ever seen do it like that. Like, 'I'm not bending, and I'm
not worried about what these white people are going to think.
I'm here and I am fashion. I'm just going to put some rollers in
my locs.' The corny people at *Jane* [didn't] get her but these people
at *Bazaar,* who are fucking dope, get it."

Dr. Yaba Blay remembers three things about 1998. It was the
year she moved back to New Orleans for graduate school after
leaving the city at age thirteen, traumatized from incidents of colorism. It was also the year *Miseducation* dropped and Sudanese su-

permodel Alek Wek appeared on the cover of *Elle* magazine. She was the darkest-skinned person ever to do so. "In fairness, I don't want to paint a picture like, 'Oh, woe is me, I've never been seen as beautiful,'" says the Ghanaian-born and NOLA-raised Blay. "Prior to Lauryn, Foxy was the redeeming person in the mainstream to validate darker brown sisters' color in a very public way. Seeing her being considered as beautiful meant that the potential existed that I could be seen as beautiful as well. But then there was this shift. Foxy was brown with a long weave. She gave you *that girl* and I loved her. But what made Lauryn Hill different from Foxy Brown to me was that Lauryn was real in a way that I could relate to. She was natural." For Blay, who'd watched Lauryn's hair grow from a short natural style with the Fugees to long locs, Lauryn offered much-needed confirmation that dark brown women with natural hair could also be considered beautiful in a way that Foxy Brown did not.

Furthermore, watching New Orleans, a city she'd known to be plagued with colorism, embrace Lauryn allayed a lot of her anxieties about moving back. "A lot of my childhood memories of New Orleans are riddled with colorism and very much wrapped up in people's negative reflections of me. The first time I heard Lauryn, I was in New Orleans, and of course, she's the hotness, and everybody's into it. Lauryn also represented some level of 'conscious' which was also encouraging." In a city that had been largely all about bounce music, Blay felt that Hill and other members of the neo-soul movement made room for other lifestyles and aesthetics. "It felt like New Orleans was catching up, so to speak." Shortly after her return to the University of New Orleans, she discovered that she might have spoken too soon. "I get there, we're rocking with Lauryn, I'm feeling good and I'm not feeling the colorism stuff as much, if at all. I'm making new friends and feeling good about myself."

And then that November Blay saw Alek Wek on the cover of *Elle*. She was delirious with excitement. "I remember, very clearly, being in the checkout line of the A&P grocery store with one of my very best male friends and when I see the magazine, I literally start jumping up and down. It was the first time I'd seen a woman [with] my complexion on the cover of a magazine and somebody was calling her beautiful." Blay was elated until she saw that her friend, who was also black, had a distinctly different reaction. "This Negro was pissed. And I was like 'What the fuck is wrong with you?'" His response was a quick and hurtful reality check.

"White people making fun of us," he said. "They know she's not beautiful." It was in that moment that Blay realized that Lauryn or no Lauryn, "We're still here. We're still here." Even still, said Blay, Lauryn meant a lot to her. And she means a lot still. "Aesthetically for sure, but she also opened up a vibe that allowed a lot of people in New Orleans to be different and to think different. To come up off the ignorance for a little and think critically about ourselves. I'm not going to lie, though. That in that moment in that A&P line . . . That shit hurt my feelings in some real ways."

I can relate. In 2001 I was the executive editor at *Essence* magazine when we made the decision to put Alek Wek on the cover. It was the 2000s and the reign of the supermodels as cover subjects was long over. That ground had been ceded to celebrities. Still, the editorial team decided the cover was both an affirmation of Wek's beauty and recognition of the pioneering role she was playing for dark-skinned black women, both within the fashion industry and out. The *Essence* fashion and beauty team, particularly dedicated to combating negative beauty narratives about black women, rose to the occasion and created one of the most stunning images of Wek to date. It was the lowest-selling issue we had that year, accompanied by copious angry letters consistent with Blay's A&P friend. It was heartbreaking and still my worst experience at the magazine in twenty years.

Alek's story is relevant here, lest anyone discount the weight of the iconic position Hill occupied. Her image wasn't just black, and it wasn't just beautiful. It was uniquely relatable in a way that allowed black women to stitch themselves into her narrative and rewrite their own. The nature of beauty being what it is, a cultural currency unfairly assigned by the luck of the genetic draw, the impact of Lauryn's beauty on other black women is rare. Beyoncé is undeniably a stunning woman but, as countless think pieces can attest, her beauty tends to be more polarizing than not. Lest this be relegated to merely light-skinned vs. dark-skinned shit, remember that Lupita Nyong'o's, Anna Wintour "It Girl" moment immediately following *12 Years a Slave* did not produce a similar phenomenon. We were able to stitch ourselves into Lauryn's narrative because she had "That Thing," that intangible every-black-girl thing that was indisputably us.

Time for a confession. It was never just how Lauryn looked. It was the way the men in hip hop looked at her, in public and with desire, that gave us hope for ourselves—especially at a time when lyrical misogyny was rapidly increasing and media reports about black women's desirability and declining marriage statistics warned us that we might be moving from waiting to exhale to simply . . . waiting. Karen Good Marable remembers the first time she ever saw Lauryn in person. "I had just moved to Brooklyn in 1993. I was with my boy 8 Ball, who was from Jersey, and Lauryn drove through Spike [Lee's] block party. She was behind the wheel, so beautiful and diminutive, in this big body truck, and my boy latched on to her window. He was like, 'I love you. I love you. I love you.'" Good Marable laughs. "He couldn't stop saying it."

Jackson remembers his first time like this: "She was as fine as cat hair, so of course I was trying to holler. But Lauryn had an ability to shift that dating energy to friendship energy easily. Part of it was that she was truly special and gifted. Before she even made records she had that kinda beauty and emotion that would elicit the best outta people." His favorite example is a run-in with the Wu-Tang Clan before the Fugees blew up. "They were leaving their gig on a bus back when buses subbed as green rooms. The Clan ran up on their bus and it was kinda dangerous for a moment, like niggas was gonna set it off. But, then they saw Lauryn," Jackson recalls, "and the energy immediately shifted to 'Yo, yo, yo. What's up shorty?' Everybody starts trying to talk to her. And Clef, he's got no wins in this because nobody's supposed to know he and Lauryn were fucking with each other. So Lauryn is just handling each motherfucker that comes at her. Left. Right. This one. That one. By the time it gets to [Ol' Dirty Bastard] the whole situation is just comical. She was able to disarm him and they just ended up having a long, quality conversation as friends. She's truly gifted in that way."

Jackson continues, "I think that for a lot of black men, Lauryn represents the love you have for your mother, for your grandmother, for your sister, for your nieces. And, also represents the sexual feminine energy that you have for your girl. You can literally see a lineage of black women in your life fucking with Lauryn. I say all of that to say she had the ability to elicit strong sorta familial urges in men in addition to sexual ones. There was a softness and a sex appeal that women respected. She [didn't] use it like a tool. She wasn't over sexualized. Women wanted [to] be like her and men wanted her. That's a big part of why it worked." For those women whose coping strategy for hip hop's growing misogyny was the kind of denial needed to convince themselves that rappers were only talking about "real" bitches and hoes—*They're not talking to me. They're talking to the women who were like that—*Lauryn was the illusion needed to fuel the fallacy that the proper amount of consciousness/righteousness/bawseness exempted you from what was obviously problematic. Of course it was a lie. No amount of #BadBitchery can inure you from the possibility of heartbreak. Don't fault us for this logic. We weren't versed yet in resisting cisgendered, heteronormative institutions steeped in patriarchy. Back then we just wanted so desperately to be chosen both by hip hop and by the men who made it. So did Lauryn. And if Hill, who was arguably the baddest pop star on the planet could have her heart broken and land on a road called Hope, then just maybe we could too. But this is a lesson each generation of women seems to have to unlearn. Cue *Lemonade* if you don't believe me.

But back to magazines.

Hands down, my favorite Lauryn Hill magazine moment was receiving the inaugural copy of *Honey* magazine with her on the cover. *Honey* was as much a product of place as it was of time, recalls cofounder Joicelyn Dingle. It was heavily influenced by Spike Lee's ungentrified Fort Greene, Brooklyn. "It was so black and something I'd never experienced, even though I'd been in other black situations. I'm from the South and I went to Hampton. It was bold and audacious and fun and sexy. Black people owned businesses. We just walked around looking like we loved ourselves. A lot." For Dingle, working as the manager for Spike Lee's store, 40 Acres and a Mule, amplified that feeling. "I saw people come from all over the country and I saw how important it was to have black things. And how much they honored Spike's work. After they bought the book, they bought the clothes. It wasn't just the store, it was the culture he helped to usher in with his films. I got to see black people who lived that way. Men who loved being black. Who loved their corner store. Who loved the dude [who] ran the corner store. It was something I fell in love with."

At this point Joicelyn and Kierna had been working on *Honey* for nearly five years. Even though the dream was still far off, they knew Lauryn was the only choice for the cover. Part of it was principle: "With *Honey* we were trying to bottle what we now understand to be black girl magic. Back then we used the language of goddess to refer to powerful black women. I think it reflected our interest and intrigue with alternate African religions that was directly related to an upsurge of cultural consciousness among black women," says Mayo. "Lauryn was an important touch point in all of that. She was the intersectionality we were looking for. In terms of our flyness, everybody wanted permission to be sexy, and hot, and fly as well as woke. All the things young women today take for granted. But it was our collective internal question mark. Which side would you choose? What could you give yourself permission to be? *Honey* was our attempt to say we are all of these things. We are intellects, we are radicals, we are fashionistas, we are wearing hot pants and red lipstick. And hip hop was this boy world that was evolving around male identity, which left us hovering around, never ever being fully centered but driving so much of the conversation. The essence of this combination was far more complex than even pop culture had recognized at that point, let alone the world. Lauryn just felt so unboxed and as women who were partaking in hip-hop culture, we needed that. We needed to be affirmed on the global stage."

Turns out the US wasn't the only place struggling with its binaries. Nadine Sutherland, a former Bob Marley protégé, a culture studies scholar and the daughter of a longtime Rasta reflects on the global impact of Lauryn's image, particularly as it pertained to black women's expressions of their sexuality: "Lauryn Hill was a culture shifter in a lot of ways, even for us here in Jamaica. Remember we are a country that still struggles with the restrictions of a patriarchal environment. She helped usher in a new school of dawtas. For young women who liked the concept of Rastafari but didn't fully buy into all of its philosophies and ideologies, Lauryn Hill gave them a different narrative. In the '70s anyone who wore dreds was a Rasta, if you saw a female reggae artist with dreadlocks, she was Rastafarian. Take for example the I-Threes, who of course were the back-up singers for Bob Marley and the Wailers.

"For a young person who was growing up in the '90s and liked that natural look but didn't want to identify as Rasta, there was really no example until Lauryn Hill. She was a conscious singer who wore dreadlocks but didn't subscribe to the orthodox practices of Rastafari women that say women must cover themselves. She was sexy, but she wasn't selling sex. She could wear a batty rider, but she wasn't overtly Babylonian. She did show some skin—God, I just remember those legs. That girl had incredible legs."

What cannot be discounted here is Hill's impact on an island that, although predominantly black, has a legacy of colorism. It always used to make me laugh that friends who hadn't been to Jamaica expected to see an island full of dreds. In the early '90s I could find more dreds on the streets in Brooklyn than I could in Jamaica. A woman who chose to cut off her hair was considered equally heretical. A woman in Kingston once hailed me up from across the road just because we both had short hair. The binary wasn't just Rasta vs. Babylon. It was that natural hair equaled being unkempt and straight hair was polished, which played into the leftover mentalities of colonization. For most of Jamaica's history, its reigning beauty standard has been mixed race or "browning." For confirmation, peep its longest-running Jamaica tourism ad featuring the honey-colored and straight-haired Trinidadian beauty Sintra Arunte-Bronte, the absence of darker-skinned women in adverts, or the ongoing choices for Miss Jamaica and Miss Universe. All are light-skinned or racially nondescript, with straight or curly hair. Consider gorgeous and un-apologetic afro-rocker Davina Bennett, the second-place runner for 2017 Miss Universe, Lauryn Hill's love child.

"She gave those young women a different imaging of what could be because of how she presented herself. In Jamaica, a lot of young women discovered a voice because of Lauryn Hill, one that allowed them to be themselves, to be sexy with a natural hairstyle. We now have a movement. Young women now feel like they can wear a nat-ural hairstyle and still be considered sexy without the ideological and religious baggage of the Rastafarian movement of the 1970s. Beau-tiful black women are wearing their hair natural and feeling confi-dent and sexy. That's because they now have a choice: they can be rootsy with long skirts and blouses that cover their elbows, or they can wear their natural hair with haute couture, or they can wear it with a batty rider in the dancehall. Our current Miss Universe wore an afro. We have Lauryn Hill and to some extent, India.Arie, to thank for that. She took our black aesthetic and made it beautiful and fashionable and sexy, and that? That helped us with the process of undoing a mind-set that taught us to hate ourselves."

In part, the decision to put Hill on the cover boiled down to access.

Lauryn was a mega enough star to launch the magazine and a

star they had access to. Joicelyn and a not-yet famous Lauryn met and became friends in Spike's store. They bonded, not surprisingly, over fashion. "She dressed like a boy, a hip-hop boy, and I didn't." Joicelyn laughs. I think she was still trying to maintain some credibility because with hip hop she was working in a very male-oriented world. "I had on a miniskirt and she was like 'I really wish I could wear stuff like that.'" Hill occasionally hosted Joicelyn's poetry readings, and Joicelyn told her that she'd like her to be the first cover. Hill agreed. But that was a '96 convo pre-'97 fame. By 1998, when the magazine was finally ready to launch, securing Lauryn got complicated in the way things do when friends get famous and have to manage label demands. Time constraints and managers, publicists and various others all have a say.

"Of course we're all friends now, but back then Jayson was giving us a really hard time. 'What is this? She can't do this. No.'" Basically he was trying not to have his client, a newly launched and very sought-after superstar, do the cover of a start-up, and the inaugural issue at that. Jayson wasn't having it, but they had already told their backers that Lauryn was a go. The situation was do or die, so in another hip-hop moment of ingenuity and black girl resourcefulness, Joicelyn did what she had to do. "One morning I said forget it. I'm calling her mama. I can't." So, very politely, she asked Mrs. Hill to put her child on the phone. "Please forgive me, but I need to speak to Lauryn. I'll be really short." Joicelyn made her case and Hill was sympathetic. She was also shooting seven covers that week and had decided this week of shooting would be her last. "Joicelyn," she confided. "I'm pregnant. Is that okay?" Joicelyn got goose bumps. She knew this was big, Joicelyn confirmed. "Are you sure?" Lauryn asked. "Lauryn, it's even better."

"But that's how we got her. We had to override the dudes. We had to override Jayson." Pregnant with her second child, she arrived at eleven on a Friday night and they got to work. With Oshun as their guide, Joicelyn executed the concept. "We had a honeycomb set, which was really like a piece of old yellow fabric with another perforated fabric under it. It gave the effect of honeycombs. We bought several jars of honey and just [put them] up and put light through [them]. And it was Friday, which is Oshun's day, so I knew we were going to be blessed. She was great, even though it was so late, and she was so tired. We didn't leave there until two or three o'clock that morning. I just appreciated her so much. She could have said no, but she knew how important it was to me. And I'd like to think that in some universal sense, she could sense how important this was for black girls."

To say representation matters is de rigueur today, but it's not just a PC matter of equal visibility. Representation matters because it allows you to grant yourself permission to become the thing you know in your heart you are but may have never seen. Says Blay, "When I started my digital campaign, PrettyPeriod I posted mad images of Lauryn. She's a symbol and an icon for many of us. I was grown, but I imagine that if I was a little dark-skinned girl at the time and seeing her on TV and people falling on the ground for her, that leaves some room open for the potential that someone could see the beauty in me as well. People say representation only matters so much, but hear me when I say that you have to see yourself reflected in a particular way to actually believe that the potential exists for you to be beautiful. Otherwise, people are gonna tell you that you're beautiful and you're not gonna believe them because you yourself don't even have a model for it. Of course, Lauryn is beautiful, of course, I'm beautiful, but if all you're seeing is light-skinned women or women who have 'mixed-girl hair' being the 'It Girls,' the video girls, the models in the magazine[s], the celebrities in the movies then you wonder where you fit in. And then you have your own people reminding you that you don't. So, Lauryn was aesthetically absolutely crucial and important to us."

Perhaps no one knows representation matters more than Michaela Angela Davis. Davis is an image activist, creative director, and cultural commentator. In the '90s she was the first fashion director at *VIBE* and the executive fashion, beauty, and culture editor at *Essence*, and she was the last editor in chief at *Honey* magazine.

Michaela Angela Davis:

My daughter Elenni said to me recently that Solange's *A Seat at the Table* was her generation's *The Miseducation of Lauryn Hill*.

JM:

Do you agree?

MAD:

There are some similarities. Like Solange, Lauryn represented what it looked like for a young, black woman to stand in all of her realness. She had a look that was political, super-stylish, and artistic. It pulled on the past and made it feel futuristic. That it still sets the bar for twentysomethings, twenty years later illustrates how that significant album was a culturally defining moment.

JM:

Why do you think that is?

MAD:

Lauryn broke through to gain "mainstream acceptance" in a way that never discounted or altered her blackness. The mainstream came to her. There was some vindication in that. It was a moment where one of our princesses got through and we were able to stand back and say, "See. This is how fresh we've always been." Now what's different between Solange's moment and Lauryn's moment has a lot to do with hair texture and skin tone—

JM:

You're talking about US colorism, right? The fact that Lauryn Hill is a dark-skinned black woman and Solange is a much lighter-complexioned one?

MAD:

Yes. Look, we know that complexion matters. No shade, but in the late '90s the significance of someone who looked like Lauryn getting the cover of *Harper's Bazaar*—as opposed to someone who looked like Solange or Beyoncé, or Rihanna, for that matter—was major.

JM:

Major. I remember being in happy shock when she landed that cover. I mean, I loved Liz Tilberis, but *Harper's Bazaar* was lily-white in those days.

MAD:

The difference between Solange and Lauryn is also in sensibility. When you compare those two album covers, for example, their approaches are radically different.

JM:

Miseducation's cover references Bob Marley's *Burnin'* album for sure.

MAD:

Yes, while *A Seat at the Table* references the *Mona Lisa*. It's beautifully done but completely inspired by Eurocentric portraiture style. The length and texture of Solange's hair and her complexion, the way she's lit and positioned, is all very Eurocentric but with this dope Solange black girl-ness pulsating throughout. Lauryn was black from the gate. I never felt like she was referencing European culture in any way. All of her fashion and beauty references were firmly rooted in blackness.

JM:

Can you remember the first time Lauryn landed on your style radar?

MAD:

It was the "Killing Me Softly" video with the Fugees, where she's sitting in that movie theater with cornrows, an afro, and a leather jacket, looking so fly. I wish I'd done a fashion editorial based on all her songs when I was a fashion editor. She was a walking editorial based on black culture, black futurism, and black radical thought. All of her style was in her songs. It was like, "here's some retro chic, here's a military thing, here's a Black Power look." Then, "here's something super glamorous and R&B." She had really good taste too, so there's that. Erykah Badu was doing this in her own way also, but Erykah was almost too much—she had ankhs, mile-high head wraps, and incense. It was almost too much juju. But Lauryn was able to smooth it all out and make it look like the dopeness we knew all black girls were.

JM:

You were a fashion editor and a stylist. Walk us through '90s black girl aesthetics. I mean Brooklyn was a mecca—Fort Greene especially. Where did Lauryn fit in? What were her style references?

MAD:

Brooklyn during the '90s was Black Bohemia central. You had mud cloth, ethnic fabrics, mixed with rock and roll. There were flowy skirts and radical tees. There was sneaker culture and natural hair and it was all smelling like frankincense and myrrh oils. Moshood on Fulton was the store. Then you'd cross the bridge into SoHo. This is when SoHo was still very, very chic. Everybody was wearing black and Japanese designers. Very Yohji Yamamoto and Comme des Garçons. Very "Oh, you're just so cool." Then you'd go up to Midtown where the Sony building was, and you'd have all the R&B queens. You'd have tight dresses, really beautiful designer shoes and super-duper makeup. Weaves were just starting to have their first big moment. The rappers Lil' Kim and Foxy Brown were [of that] moment but with a hypersexualized, in-your-face kind of sexy.

JM:

Hip hop's ghetto fabulous, bling moment. Gucci, Prada, Balenciaga, Louboutin, Louis Vuitton . . .

MAD:

Yes. But with here's my ass and I'm squatting in your face.

JM:

When it came to music and fashion, Lauryn was a diasporic chameleon in terms of style and aesthetics. Where did you root her?

MAD:

To me, Lauryn registered as East Coast black American and West Indian—Jamaican specifically. Lauryn was a Jersey black girl who definitely repped where she came from, but she was clearly influenced by a Jamaican, Ethiopian, and African moment that was happening in the late '90s. She had Afrocentric sensibilities, but they were pushed through a Jamaican lens. She brought Bob Marley to the cookout. But it's interesting, I think Lauryn was much more influenced by Bob Marley and men's fashion than she was [by] Rita Marley or the I-Threes. She wasn't wearing long skirts or sundresses. She was wearing those beautiful, fitted military jackets and jeans. She looked to Marley as a muse. But Lauryn also fucked with you in that way. Back then, to have locs made you a roots girl. If you wore them with a long skirt you were a Rasta. And modest. Lauryn was not modest.

In some ways, Lauryn defined a new category for us because her body was the intersection of so many different black girl aesthetics. What made her fascinating was the way she signaled these multiple spaces of blackness in her style. She could signal her hip hop, signal her glamour, and signal her sexy—sometimes all at the same time. She pulled them all together and made it work.

JM:

How? Because not everyone can do that.

MAD:

Part of the reason it worked was that her actual body—the canvas on which these clothes were placed—was also a site of intersecting identities. She brought all these black girls together in her body. Anything you put on her was going to be activated differently than if it was on a Beyoncé, who's dope in her own right, but her body just doesn't do that. There were definitely dope black female artists with signature styles in the '90s—Aaliyah, Sade—but they were all giving you one look. One note. One mood. Lauryn exemplified our complexity and how those complexities could complement each other. Black women are dynamic. We can be sexy. And tomboy. And radical. And church girl. And visionary. With wizardry. Lauryn knew that. All of these different elements intersected on her actual black body and she made them all cooler. What she did was very hard to do, and she made it look effortless. That's the reason she became such a style influence, and the reason she's so hard to replicate.

JM:

Let's talk about Lauryn as a beauty girl. I've been looking at a lot of old images of her and I'm struck by how on trend her look is right now. Dewy skin, highly pigmented and glitter eyeshadows, shiny lip glosses. I mean, Lauryn was rocking a black lip back in the '90s.

MAD:

You know, Joan, it's only been in the last five years that we've been talking about radiant, glowing skin. Throughout the late '80s to mid early 2000s it was all about 'Matte that shit down.' Foundation was used to perform surgery. You would go to a video shoot and they would have a spray gun. That was the airbrush era. Real talk. Every makeup artist had an airbrush gun and the directive was to make the skin the same color. Lauryn was one of the few people where you could see her actual skin—

JM:

As opposed to a mask of make-up.

MAD:

Lauryn was a bit of a fashion historian. She had a retro chic that made you think she was probably studying black beauty aesthetics of the '70s and '80s. This is when you could turn on *Soul Train* on the TV or look at *Ebony* and *Essence* magazines to see beautiful, glowing, radiant black skin in different shades. All you needed was some lip gloss and mascara. Lauryn was giving that very early. Sometimes she just wore a great lip, skin, and eyelashes. Remember twenty years ago, you had to go get your momma's or your auntie's "Raisin" by Fashion Fair to get that dark lip because not even MAC was poppin' like that. I feel like Lauryn was pulling out her "Raisin" and giving it a darker lip line to make it modern. When you look at the "Doo Wop" video, she looks like she stepped right out of 1978, and yet it wasn't corny. Why? Because she knew how to do that thing.

JM:

What was the significance of her videos, visually speaking?

MAD:

Her videos were so important because they were style in motion.
Every time you saw her on a moped she looked fly, sexy, and
free. But she looked like a free radical. Lauryn's music was
political—she talked about racism, gender dynamics, capitalism,
and she gave those politics a look. What made her look political
was that she dared to be intersectional. She dared to be sexy
and military and radical and retro and chic all at the same time.
That was revolutionary for the time. And I miss that because
this fucking pink hat . . .

JM:

Her autonomy is interesting when you consider that the '90s
marks the rise of the celebrity stylist. We started to see a lot less
individuality and personal style from artists—from hip hop to
Hollywood. We still see fashion, of course, but the stylist becomes
the interpreter. And everybody used one.

MAD:

Yes. In music, that happened partially because of the rise of
video culture and introduction of the Internet. The stylist of the

day in hip hop was June Ambrose. June was the queen. She was dressing everybody back then and she was making them look *hot*. She still is. But here's the thing, nobody dressed Lauryn. This I know for a fact. When it came to putting together her looks, you worked for her. You shopped for her. She would say, "I want you to help me find a fitted military jacket." Or she would tell you this was a leather moment. She didn't come to magazines or stylists and say, "Okay, now do me." She came and said "I'm here. Let's see what you have that works for me." You were her staff. Or her consultant. But she was her own muse.

Let me clarify that. Overall, I think Lauryn's muse was blackness: black people, the black community, black history, black politics, black thought. When you are pulling on blackness in such a full way, you don't need anybody to tell you what to wear. You just need them to help you get the visual proof of it.

JM:

Let's talk hair. In 2018, it's common to see black women rocking natural hair. Black models are wearing natural hair in everything from commercials to high fashion advertisements. Saint Laurent has black girls rocking cornrows. Gucci has black girls with short natural fros. The models Philomena Kwao and Adwoa Aboah are out here killing it. Not to mention a natural-hair industry that is estimated conservatively to be worth 2.56 billion dollars in

2016. This is not where we were in 1998. It was a struggle to even get good products. There were no YouTube tutorials to guide you through. You relied on shared knowledge between the few women who'd also "gone natural" or you went to the barber and got a caesar so low that maintenance didn't matter. Lauryn got to the party early.

MAD:

The party wasn't even close to starting. Lauryn entered with natural hair. Even before she had locs, she wore cornrows and afros, twists and coils. She showed us the versatility, resilience, and shape-shifting of black hair. That first *Honey* magazine cover? Oh my God.

JM:

It's iconic.

MAD:

In the same way that *VIBE* magazine cover with Treach is iconic. It was like *fuck*. That's it. That's how hot we are. I wanted to take that *Honey* cover with Lauryn and just run around the street and show it to everybody saying "See! See! See!" She had locs and she was beautiful, glamorous, and sexy all at the same time. It was radical. But then by the same token you could also see her with a straight wig and yet none of her beauty references fell outside of blackness.

That was really a power shift because the fashion world was so exclusive and elite back then. Remember, there was no Instagram, Tumblr, or Pinterest. There were no independent spaces where you could show the full breadth of black women's aesthetics. Lauryn Hill was our Pinterest. She was our Instagram. She made people contend with black beauty in a way that no one else had.

JM:

I'm glad you said that. Lauryn Hill, for me, is the visual precursor to #BlackGirlMagic. This generation owes her their inheritance.

MAD:

Absolutely. She gave this generation permission. Permission to have a caesar one day and a long, silky weave on another. Or a radical beret on one day and sparkly short shorts on the next. To be a fucking warrior one day and magical and whimsical on another. She taught us that all you had to do to pull it off was to bring all your black girl-ness to all of it. That was her

gift to us. She was the one who broke through and she got a
bit broken in the journey.

JM:

It's important to honor that because so much focus is put on
the fact that there was never a successful album from her after
Miseducation when Lauryn's contribution is so much bigger
than just one album.

MAD:

There's still a constant push for black women and girls to be
contained. Like you can occupy one lane but don't fuck with
this other stuff—

JM:

But we can occupy your lane whenever we want and never
acknowledge the origins or the creators.

MAD:

Right. Lauryn showed the world what black girls can do and
that others simply can't. Kylie Jenner can't fucking ever look like
Lauryn Hill. That's triggering to some people.

JM:

That's because there's a difference between creating culture and appropriating culture. Shade intended.

MAD:

And Lauryn created culture and she studied it. She went deep into Jamaican culture. She went deep into '70s black aesthetics. She went deep into R&B and soul. She helped redefine hip-hop culture. She was so culturally and philosophically sound that you couldn't fuck with her. And you couldn't duplicate her because her foundation was so strong. She wasn't just throwing trends at you. You could never identify her as trendy. Ever. She defined shit. She was the remixer. Like . . . she was hip hop. Or she was the best of what hip hop could be. Male, female, black, white, whatever. Take all the races and all the genders. She rocked the party and gave you shit to think about. She was political. She was sexy. Lauryn Hill was the fucking love song.

The late '90s [were] an exciting time in hip-hop, one that was coming off of a very violent period. It was a very musical time. D'Angelo, Erykah Badu, Common, and of course, Lauryn were on one end of the spectrum and blunts and Hennessy straight out the bottle were another. It was a powerful turn for the culture because we had all of these different energies coming out of hip hop and converging. Prior to that, hip hop was thought of as primarily East Coast and West Coast, but in the '90s that changed. You had Missy [Elliot] and Timbaland coming out of Virginia, Organized Noize, OutKast, that Dallas Austin production coming out of the South, and Lil Wayne and Juvenile coming out of New Orleans. All of these different worlds were coming together and demanding space. But the violence was real. As much as I want to remember the '90s fondly when I listen to some of the lyrics, now it's like "Damn. We were all kinds of bitches and hoes."

I think it's important to remember the climate Missy, Erykah, and Lauryn entered in. They came in counter to this violence and extreme misogyny. The ways Missy used and represented her body in her videos defied definition. She challenged you at every turn. Erykah was something we'd never seen before—that combination of 5 percenter, Queen Afua earth mother. And then you had Lauryn. She was amazing. She could rhyme. She could sing. She was beautiful to look at. And she took herself seriously at that time when we, as women in hip hop, needed that. We needed to see this deeply chocolate woman with such a command of her body, who could sing and rhyme as well as any of these boys . . . She also made herself really vulnerable in the music. We needed that too.

—*Karen Good Marable*

3 / '90s Kind of Love

It was the summer of '98 and New York City streets were not only hot, they were buzzing. L-Boogie's highly anticipated, first Fugee-free joint had finally arrived. Its mission was made clear from the merciless syncopation of its opening bars: "*It's Funny how money change a situation/Miscommunication leads to complication.*" Not only had Lauryn Hill not come to play, she'd launched a sonic missile from her new address on Hope Road—one that landed with blinding precision at the feet of wherever Wyclef was that summer when he first heard "Lost Ones." It scorched the earth around him like a bomb.

But Wyclef wasn't the only intended target. *The Miseducation of Lauryn Hill* arrived in the world embattled, fighting for its life after a critical failure to launch. The factors at play were multiple. First there was a long-standing agreement between the Fugees that they would each release solo records without disbanding the group—and that they would support one another in the endeavor. Capitalizing on the success of *The Score*, Wyclef released *The Carnival* in 1997, and true to her word, Hill has writing, vocal, and production credit. While Hill waited for Clef to return the favor, Pras released "Ghetto Superstar" in 1998, followed by John Forte's "Poly Sci." Still nothing.

There's no question that the deterioration of Hill and Wyclef's romantic and professional relationships were a contributing factor. Those details won't be parsed here. Suffice it to say that love triangles are messy and the twenties are a decade punctuated with messes to which twentysomethings are entitled. Lauryn and Wyclef were not the first couple to fuel the intensity of the creative process with a volatile cocktail of passion, talent, drama, ambition, love, and sex, and they certainly won't be the last. There is something to be said for the differences in the manner each of them chose to lick those wounds. Lauryn gave the public no details and documented her journey through her art, in an album that twenty years later qualifies as a classic and has now given two generations a vehicle for healing. Wyclef chose *The Wendy Williams Show* and a tell-all memoir, *Purpose: An Immigrant's Story*, choices that will forever condemn his version of their story as sensationalist gossip.

Eventually, Hill was no longer willing to wait. She coaxed Jackson to leave his position as head of marketing at Bad Boy Records and become her full-time manager. It was a calculated risk for both of them. "Nineteen ninety-six and '97 were the hottest years that pop would ever see," explains Jackson, who was at a label responsible for the successes of hit-makers including the late Craig "Flava in Ya Ear" Mack, Carl Thomas, Sean Combs, Faith Evans, and The Notorious B.I.G. Lauryn was also at a crossroads. There was the safety of success and the Fugees were at the height of it. In addition to record-breaking sales, they were touring extensively and making good money while doing it. But Lauryn was also pregnant, beefing with Clef, and miserable. Looking back, Jackson thinks that she started writing songs partially as a coping mechanism. "Lauryn would call a lot from the road. One of the first songs that she played for me was 'Zion.' She'd written about half of it, called me and sang it to me over the phone." As soon as Jackson heard it, he knew it was time for both of them to make money moves—not only for their respective careers but also for the sake of Hill's emotional and creative health. "There's a saying that goes 'the next best thing to having sex with a woman is making money with her.' That was the relationship and the energy that existed between [me and] Lauryn. It wasn't about it being sexual. She was as thirsty to smash the whole game as I was to be an agent in helping her smash it." When Hill asked him what he thought of the song, Jackson's answer was blunt. "I was like, 'Oh my God! Leave the group. Bail. You need to be making great music.'" Jackson soon followed suit, threw security to the wind, and left his marketing position at the label.

It was no easy endeavor, for Hill or for Jackson. First, there were the months of creative labor—a process made even more strenuous by the emotional toll of the whirlwind of a bitter breakup, a new relationship with Rohan Marley, and a subsequent pregnancy all happening in a relatively brief window of time. To add to that stress, Hill, determined to protect both her privacy and her unborn child, took great lengths to keep both the relationship and her pregnancy out of the public eye and away from much of her intimate circle. Even Jackson didn't know. Radio personality Wendy Williams, who'd built a controversial career throughout the '90s spilling celebrity tea (the more salacious the better), was the first to break the news during an interview Jackson classifies as an ambush. "At that point, no one knew. As close as we were, even I didn't know. I don't even know if Lauryn's parents knew, quite honestly. People were still trying to get confirmation on Clef and Lauryn's relationship. Hell, there were people who thought Lauryn and I were dating." Hill was shocked but remained gracious and composed. She confirmed that she was pregnant, but the father's identity was something she chose to keep to herself. News quickly spread, and the reaction, by both the public and those close to her, was less than supportive. Hill was twenty-two and at what people then thought was the height of her career. Very few thought the move could be anything more than burdensome: *Look at your career, they said/ Lauryn baby, use your head/But instead I chose to use my heart.*

Instead, it became "To Zion," an anthem for motherhood, choice, and one of her most popular songs—eventually. Initially, not everyone was moved, including her label.

Hill took "To Zion" and a few other songs from the album-to-be to a meeting with Columbia's brass. Tommy Mottola, then-head of Sony Music and Entertainment, pronounced it dead on arrival. Mottola was anxious to replicate the Fugees' success and thought this new mélange of soul, reggae, and relatively little hip hop from one of rap's best emcees was too much of a departure from a proven formula. "They weren't feeling it at all," says Jackson. "Basically, they wanted a Fugees record without the guys. Tommy told her that it was a smoky little ditty, but it wasn't her. Go back and try again. She came out of that meeting crying. The record was so personal to her. His reaction crushed her."

Hill was hurt but she wasn't defeated. No one on her management team thought that the album as she'd conceived it was dead, but they agreed that the label's reaction definitely had it lingering in the intensive care unit. "I mean, looking back I can see Tommy's point," Jackson concedes with the benefit of hindsight. "The Fugees were the biggest-selling rap group at the time, and it makes sense that they would want to do it again, but at the time that's not how I saw it. Back then I was like, 'Fuck him. We don't need them. This is what we gonna do.'"

Jackson and the team's inside playa, Suzette Williams, who was both an executive at the label and part of Hill's management team, devised a resuscitation plan. Taking Mottola's advice, they decided to try something else, but the strategy was hardly what he could have wanted. In an act of sheer hip-hop hustle and ingenuity, they took the hardest and the most signature L-Boogie rap track on the album and hand-delivered "Lost Ones" to Ruffhouse Records cofounder Chris Schwartz. Schwartz did his bit for history and agreed to press a limited number on twelve-inch vinyl so they could distribute to mix shows and club deejays.

It was a brilliant move. In a genre where the battle record is a revered staple, this one brought the fire. Beautiful and bellicose, "Lost Ones" not only showcased the best of Lauryn's skills as an emcee, it was so purely hip hop that it appealed directly to her original fan base, letting them know she hadn't abdicated the temple of their familiar. It was also froggy as fuck. Peppered with rude gyal-isms and a reggae assist from Sister Nancy's classic "Bam Bam," Hill, ironically, had achieved Clef's original mission, the one he'd wanted to accomplish with the Fugees "Killing Me Softly." "Lost Ones" killed the sound bwoy dead.

Be it on the radio or in the club, there wasn't a deejay worth her salt who didn't include "Lost Ones" somewhere in her set. DJ Belinda Becker remembers that summer well. "As a deejay you just knew that at the height of the night, when the hip hop was pumping, 'Lost Ones' was the one to slam on. The minute that first beat dropped, the crowd would just go crazy. Everybody knew the lyrics. It's just a dance floor mover," says Becker. "Always, always, always. I think Lauryn knew that in addition to the singing she also had to be able to go hard," she continues. "Especially at that time, because as a female emcee you weren't just up against female emcees. You were also up against people like Mobb Deep."

It also addressed long-standing curiosities regarding the real status of Clef and Lauryn's relationship. "Essentially," says Jackson. "It was everything [the] streets wanted to hear."

Even today, "it's still in the top 100 of greatest songs for a deejay to play when you're losing the crowd. It's one of those songs that the crowd knows within the first three seconds, even if they aren't music heads. That initial *boom bap bah boom bap*? That's it. Then she had the nerve to pause and hit it again. *Boom bap bah boom bap.* Then she layers on that bass? From the very first line, you just know it's going down."

It was the '90s equivalent of a viral sensation. "Lost Ones" was not only the fiyah that spread everywhere, it created the demand for more. Officially the phoenix rising from the ashes, "Lost Ones" had won the war by forcing Columbia's hand. *Miseducation* was released shortly after in July 1998 to record-breaking success, which exceeded even the Fugees.

"In terms of hip hop? Line for line, verse for verse 'Lost Ones' is a top-25 classic and will be forever," says Schott Free, in part because it provided the perfect vehicle for catharsis, and in exquisite hip-hop fashion. It was the kind of track you listened to when your baser nature wanted to fuck someone up but your saner self would rather not risk jail. "Music, particularly hip hop, for me is a way for me not to indulge in that response," explains Free. "Rather than punch you in your face, I can go sit down, listen to a record and get just as much of a release. 'Lost Ones,'" he concludes, "is a mood record. You listen to it when you're mad that someone's not keeping it 100. It's a character check."

Battle records are common in hip hop, but what was also unique about "Lost Ones" was the quality of Hill's rage. Its source of inspiration might have been a broken heart, but it was wholly unlike the gendered expressions traditionally assigned to female artists, especially in soul and R&B. It was completely sans tears or pleading. On the contrary, it was an exercise in precision. Hill's delivery was calm, measured, and focused on her target. With each hypercontrolled lyric, she took her power back. Free agrees. "She's not happy in 'Lost Ones,' but she's also not crying.

She's not moaning and she's not whining. You're basically getting her anger." And with it a rare opportunity for the cathartic release hip hop is known for, but one usually associated with testosterone. For female hip-hop fans, especially those with more bellicose tendencies, it was a win made even more delicious by the fact that it sampled another female artist. Lynnée Denise is still awed: "I mean, you go into the crates, pull out Sister Nancy, rearrange it to get a very specifically sped-up version and produce that?! This was not a game. This was a call to action. This was Lauryn's machete rhyme. She's telling you that she will cut you." The fact that it was easy to dance to was also unique because it allowed the catharsis to be not just mental but physical. It's a moment we've yet to be seen replicated by a female rapper, even twenty years later, although the moment has its pop culture equivalents. "It's that moment in *Waiting to Exhale* when Angela Bassett sets her husband's clothes on fire and walks away from her burning home," Lynnée Denise says, laughing. Or that moment in "Hold Up" when Beyoncé is smashing windshields with a baseball bat, smiling just as pretty as she pleases. All kudos to "Ether," Remy Ma's lyrical massacre of Nicki Minaj, for being one of the best lyrical battle moments of the twenty-first century, however the track wasn't meant to be danceable. "Lost Ones" offered the whole package. Or as crunk feminist scholar Dr. Brittney Cooper would say, it was a black girl's most eloquent rage.

That reactions to Hill's pregnancy were mixed is not surprising. Navigating the fraught relationship between motherhood and career is an ongoing staple of both feminism and contemporary womanhood. In the 1960s, a good three decades before Hill's pregnancy, seminal Black Arts Movement writers Sonia Sanchez and Alice Walker both dealt with unsolicited speculations about their ability to be mothers and successfully continue doing "the work." It was presumed "the work" would stop, Lynnée Denise explains. "Evidently they were surrounded by folks who equated motherhood with a kind of sloth." And when they didn't stop working, "they were demonized for not being maternal enough." These attitudes are particularly true of industries that are male-dominated. "I did a comparative look at Nina Simone and Lauryn Hill," Lynnée Denise said. "When Nina got pregnant in 1961 with her daughter, Lisa, the record company told her they would have to hide the pregnancy. They were like, 'No. Women don't have children this early in their careers.' That Lauryn came back almost forty years later and said, 'The record company told me not to do this,' is really important because it speaks to the toxic Harvey Weinstein environment that the music industry functions in and its attitudes around gender."

Valid point, but the negative reactions to Hill's pregnancy can't all simply be relegated to good ol' boy sexism. Twenty years later those attitudes haven't disappeared, and many of them are held by women. Despite rapper Cardi B's gorgeous and relatively well-received baby bump reveal during her April 2018 *Saturday Night Live* performance, there was plenty of online criticism from women who questioned the wisdom of having a child at a high point in her early career. The twenty-five-year-old rapper shared her disappointment in an April 11 episode of radio station Hot 97's morning show *The Breakfast Club*. "It really bothers me and disgusts me," she said. "I see a lot of women online like, 'Oh, I feel sorry for you. Oh, your career is over.' And it's like, why can't I have both? As a woman, why can't I have both? Why do I gotta choose a career or a baby? I want both." She positioned her choice as not only a personal one, "I just didn't want to deal with the whole abortion thing," but a responsible one that she was more than equipped to handle. "You know what, I'm a grown woman. I'm twenty-five years old. I'm gonna say this in the most humblest way: I'm a shmillionaire. And I'm prepared for this."

Most of the women I asked to share their initial reactions to Hill's pregnancy remembered being less than enthused. Some of those responses were certainly classed and shaped by a good dose of respectability politics. For many fans, Lauryn was seen as the desirable antidote to Lil' Kim and Foxy Brown's hypersexuality. A smart, hyperarticulate Ivy Leaguer who came from a two-parent home, Hill was the kind of "good" black girl who didn't have a baby out of wedlock. Even self-professed feminists remembered feeling concerned that the demands of motherhood would throw Hill way off her game, at a time when the world was just starting to open up for her. By the time she was pregnant with her second baby, Selah, there was a lot of "Girl, what are you doing?" going on.

Akiba Solomon definitely remembers having questions. "To be honest, I had very serious trouble relating to the idea that if you get pregnant at a time that isn't convenient that you just won't get an abortion," she shared. "The first baby, I had mixed feelings about. A woman should be able [to do] what she needs to do with her body but I did feel like 'To Zion' and the whole feeling around the song negated the idea that abortions were available and that black women can and do have them. What I didn't realize at that time but what came into sharper relief was that Lauryn was also chasing a culture that was not an African American culture," Solomon continued. "When she was with the Fugees it was like, 'Okay, I'm chasing Haitian culture.' Then it was a fascination with Jamaican culture and Rastafarianism. By the second pregnancy I started feeling like 'Is she just doing this to keep this Marley boy that nobody's ever heard of?'"

"People fucking turned on her, inside and outside of the community and the music industry. And that had to play a role in her emotional health," says Lynnée Denise. I'm not sure it was that simple. In the '90s black women were squeezed between competing narratives. Mainstream feminism still championed the idea that women should be able to have it all. "It" being career, marriage, great sex, kids, etc. Of course, the whole thing was very cisgendered and none of it has questioned marriage itself as an institution or what viable families can look like outside those heteronormative models—but this was mid-2000s talk. The '90s was the era of *Waiting to Exhale*. There was so much pressure for black women. The pressure to get chosen. The pressure not to be a statistic. The pressure to do it the "right" way, all the while well-publicized stats on drastic declines in marriage for black women constantly reminded us that having the option was increasingly a statistical improbability. These are the 1990s numbers that sounded the alarm: An estimated 25 percent of black women will never marry, a rate three times below that of white women. In 1990 only 39.4 percent of black families with children were two-parent households. These doomsday reports about marriage stats being on an increasing decline for black women would eventually become twisted narratives about black women being unmarriage-able that emerged in the early 2000s. And undesirable. (#FuckSteveHarvey)

As it turns out, in 2018, much of those anxieties were justified. The '90s is when black women went from *Waiting to Exhale* to just . . . waiting. In her book, *Eloquent Rage: A Black Feminist Discovers her Superpower*, Brittney Cooper reports the following: "Sometimes I run the numbers in my head, but this, too, is a

double-edged sword. When I see the abysmal state of black love by
the numbers, it's hard to blame myself. It's hard to have any sense
of hope either. Only 49 percent of black women with a college
degree marry men with some post-secondary education. Fifty-
eight percent of black women college graduates marry men with
an overall level of education that they have. Moreover, more than
60 percent of black women college graduates between the ages of
twenty-five and thirty-five, peak childbearing years, have never
been married. Compare that number with a mere 38 percent of
white women overall for whom this is true . . . Black women who
have never married outnumber black men who have never married at a rate of 100 to 92." Statistics, however, don't tell the full
story. In order to fully understand the emotional resonance that
Miseducation holds for black women, both then and now, requires
revisiting when and where it entered. *The Miseducation of Lauryn Hill* was born between two love triangles, the personal one
between Hill, Wyclef Jean, and his fiancée, and a political one
between a married President, his wife, and a White House intern.

Bill Clinton arrived in the presidential arena as a saxophone-
playing, forty-six-year-old baby boomer and a liberal Democrat
whose campaign ushered in an optimism and youthfulness about
the future. His early presidency, however, was quickly mired in
a rapid succession of controversies, political failures, and scandal. Among them was a failed attempt at health reform, sexual

harassment accusations, and, perhaps most damning, the White-water scandal, a botched real estate deal that hinted at financial impropriety and accusations of a cover-up. The latter turned into a formal investigation led by a particularly rabid special prosecutor named Ken Starr. Clinton became Starr's white whale. When Clinton managed to emerge from Whitewater with his presidency still intact, Starr turned his full attention to allegations of an affair between the president and a White House intern named Monica Lewinsky. The president's decision to lie about it was an act Starr, contrary to the opinions of most Americans and the rest of the free world, considered an impeachable offense. Starr failed to topple the presidency, of course, but the cumulative conflama left Clinton scurrying to regain the political capital necessary to secure a second term. How did he do it? By deploying a political strategy that turned the black women who comprised part of his base into sacrificial lambs: Clinton the liberal morphed into Clinton the moderate. Shifting sharply to the right, the embattled president continued to jack the Republican agenda by implementing two key pieces of legislation that not only had devastating effects on black women, but also destabilized the social conditions necessary for healthy black relationships to flourish for decades to come.

Dr. Treva Lindsey, a hip-hop feminist and Ohio State Associate Professor of Women's, Gender, and Sexuality Studies, marvels at the irony. "It's always intriguing to me how much love the Clintons, particularly Bill Clinton, gets from black women, because so many of his policies both indirectly and directly attack[ed] the livelihood and lives of black women in the '90s." Two pieces of legislation in particular demonstrate this: the Violent Crime Control and Law Enforcement Act of 1994 and the Personal Responsibility and Work Opportunity Reconciliation Act of 1996, otherwise known colloquially as the "Three Strikes Bill" and "Welfare to Work," respectively.

The history of the Three Strikes Bill is as follows, reports Thomas Frank in a *Guardian* article entitled, "Bill Clinton's Crime Bill Destroyed Lives and There's No Point Denying It": "Back in the early 1990s, and although they were chemically almost identical, crack and powder cocaine were regarded very differently by the law. The drug identified with black users (crack) was treated as though it were 100 times as villainous as the same amount of cocaine, a drug popular with affluent professionals. This 'now-notorious 100-to-one' sentencing disparity, as *The New York Times* put it, had been enacted back in 1986, and the 1994 crime law instructed the US Sentencing Commission to study the subject and adjust federal sentencing guidelines as it saw fit."

The Sentencing Commission duly recommended that the 100-to-1 sentencing disparity be abolished, largely because (as their lengthy report on the subject puts it) "The 100-to-1 crack cocaine to powder cocaine quantity ratio is a primary cause of the growing disparity between sentences for black and white federal defendants." By the time their report was released, however, Republicans had gained control of Congress, and they passed a bill explicitly overturning the decision of the Sentencing Commission.

The bill then went to President Clinton for approval. Two weeks after publicly delivering a speech supporting the findings of the Sentencing Commission, Clinton blithely affixed his signature to the bill "retaining the 100-to-1 sentencing disparity, a disparity that had brought about the lopsided incarceration of black people. Clinton could have vetoed it, but he didn't. He signed it."

While the Three Strikes Bill is routinely discussed in terms of mass incarceration and the legislation's damaging impact on black men, its impact on black women is given considerably less attention. Black women were deeply affected by the War on Drugs in ways that started with the Reagan and Bush agendas and continued under Bill Clinton throughout the 1990s. Drug laws began targeting nonviolent offenders and hitting them with mandatory minimum sentences. According to Amnesty International, in 1997, 138,000 women served time as a result of the War on Drugs. This is because police officers arrested not only drug dealers, but also addicts, their wives, and their lovers. Beginning in 1985, female prisoner population grew at a rate of 11.1 percent, which was higher than the 7.9 percent increase in male prisoners. From 1986–1996, the number of women's state facilities increased by 888 percent. Black women were 46 percent of the prison population. The number of women in state prisons increased between 1985 and 1991 by 828 percent for black women vs. 241 percent for white women.

"What this does in terms of black women," says Lindsey, "is literally destroy families. In addition to incarcerating them at obscene rates, it also leaves black women not only as single-headed households but it also leaves them seeing their fathers, uncles, romantic partners, friends—their communities—largely decimated for drug offenses and drug use." It had a disparate impact on black women not only because more black women went to jail, she explains, but also because of the position black women held as economic providers in their families. Nineties' job prospects also experienced a severe decline, due to another Clinton initiative called the North American Free Trade Agreement (NAFTA) that created zones in places like the Caribbean to basically provide sweatshop labor to American corporations that were exempted from basic labor requirements like standard wages. "As these jobs are moved out of the country," says Lindsey, "black women, who used to work two or three of these lower-income jobs to make ends meet, find it increasingly difficult to find work."

But while NAFTA and the Three Strikes Bill impacted black women in ways that were deleterious but, at least in terms of intent, incidental, the Personal Responsibility and Work Opportunity Reconciliation Act seemed deliberately targeted and personal. Black women found themselves on the losing end of several winning acts of political genius that capitalized on sentiments established by Daniel Patrick Moynihan's notorious 1965 study "The Negro Family: The Case For National Action." Often cited, the study erroneously blamed single black women and poor parenting skills for the alleged pathologies of the black community. Clinton capitalized on American's long-standing unease about welfare queens and tendencies to cast black women as the system's greatest abusers, despite the statistical reality that the majority of welfare recipients are actually white. "Sixty-one percent of the population receiving welfare, listed as 'means-tested cash assistance' by the Census Bureau, is identified as white," wrote Barbara Ehrenreich in a 2001 *Time* magazine article entitled "Welfare. A White Secret." "Only 33 percent is identified as black."

The title of the bill itself was a diabolical-but-effective act of political framing, explains Rutgers University Assistant Professor of Africana Studies, Dr. Akissi Britton. "The very name of the 1996 act illustrates how politicians and citizens, both Republican and Democrat, viewed the persistence of poverty. The title of the act states that the bill would bring poor people's personal responsibility in line with their work opportunities. The act focused on intervening in the personal lives of the poor (especially poor black women) to rehabilitate their deviant cultural behaviors." According to Britton, Clinton successfully drew on changing perceptions about poverty that had been in play for at least forty years. "The shifting narrative reframed poverty as the outcome of pathological cultural behaviors rather than as the result of economic and political policies that further entrenched poverty in inner-city areas," says Britton. "Supported by the 'culture of poverty' thesis—which argued that persistent poverty was the result of poor morals, debauched values, and deviant cultural behaviors—politicians campaigned on the idea that the government was being defrauded by people who refused to work, eschewed marriages, and had multiple children in order to get aid from the government. This ideology was buoyed by the image of the 'welfare queen,' a black unwed mother with multiple babies collecting checks from the government while refusing to work, which was used by Ronald Reagan in his 1976 presidential campaign. Welfare fraud became the defining argument of the reframing of poverty that was used to justify slashing government support of struggling citizens during a time when the US economy was in decline."

Even the signing of the bill was a well-orchestrated act of political theater at black women's expense. "When Clinton signed the bill, he trotted out Lillie Harden, a black Arkansas woman who had been unemployed and dependent on welfare benefits," Britton continues. "As part of the program Clinton put in place as governor of Arkansas, Harden stated that taking part in the state's welfare-to-work programs gave both her and her children a sense of pride in her new role as a wage earner." What neither

Clinton, Harden, or the rest of the bill's supporters made clear that day was that PRWORA would require those recipients to take part in the new "welfare-to-work" programs that primarily consisted of jobs too low-paying to survive on, effectively preventing recipients from managing their households. They did, however, states Britton, "provide government contractors with an abundant source of low-wage workers."

For black women especially, Welfare to Work was Clinton's Trojan horse. It imposed work-activity sanctions and family cap policies if work activity requirements weren't met. Black women were kicked off welfare rolls at higher rates than whites, while white women received more work support. The work support built into the bill did include childcare assistance, transportation, and job training but it was implemented unequally, leaving a gap in assistance to black women. Family cap policies also meant children born after the mother began receiving welfare benefits didn't receive support, again disproportionately affecting black women. Racism also meant that employment opportunities weren't always equal. Overall, employers looked less favorably at hiring black welfare recipients than white ones.

The act also cut provisions that had been critical in social advancement. Under AFDC (Assistance for Families with Dependent Children), welfare recipients with high school diplomas were more likely to attend college than nonrecipients. Under Welfare to Work, AFDC was cut and replaced with TANF (Temporary Assistance to Needy Families). TANF welfare recipients were less likely to attend college. In addition, under TANF rules college enrollment was not considered valid work activity, reducing college attendance by welfare recipients. Welfare to Work also placed a lifetime ban on people convicted of a state or federal drug offense, which prevented them from receiving cash assistance and food stamps. According to the Sentencing Project, this ban affected more than 92,000 women and 135,000 children, half of whom were black or Latina. Immigrants were affected too. Under the new bill, immigrants were now ineligible to receive welfare for their first five years in the country, the period when they were likely to need it the most.

"It was a heartless bill," says Lindsey. "Three of [Clinton's] assistant secretaries at Health and Human Services resigned in protest." In light of these political and social realities, Zion, both the child and the song, feels more and more like a revolutionary act. Black women rarely get credit for the strength it takes to choose motherhood in the face of both stigma and what the rest of society considers imperfect circumstances. "Black motherhood is maligned on one hand, and an impossible category for black women to occupy in 'the right way' on another," says Lindsey. The right way. Fast-forward twenty years and I've spent a lot of time holding hands of girlfriends who waited for "the right way" to manifest and the heartbreak of realizing "the right way" was a perpetual no-show. The pain that comes with having to accept that the realization that the children you always took for granted that you would "just have" is no longer a biological possibility? That's real. Lindsey agrees. "As black women, we're offered a very limited range of choices based on our structural realities. For black women, so often reproductive justice and choice is talked about in terms of the ways we decide not to have children. But in order for real reproductive justice and choice to exist, we also have to talk more honestly about how black women are also talked out of becoming mothers." It makes sense that "To Zion" became an anthem for so many black women, especially those who found themselves making the decision to become mothers while facing "imperfect" circumstances. "There was something so powerful about Lauryn, a black woman who [made] a defiant choice about how she was going to do black motherhood," says Lindsey, "because everything, politically and personally, was telling her that she shouldn't." Lynnée Denise agrees. "That song has been affirming for so many children, period, but especially for black children. My neighbor actually named her son Zion. He grew up listening to that song."

And yet, there are so many ways it could have gone left. Strongly evangelistic with distinctly gospel overtones, it could have been the perfect pro-life track and yet Hill beautifully and vulnerably created a vehicle that tenderly supports choice. This is a

testimony to the wisdom of Hill's choices, starting with her choice
in vocal arrangement. "She stays in a tenor almost the whole time,
when we're used to hearing her in alto," Lynnée Denise remarks.
It's a decision that conveys another level of vulnerability. "She un-
derstands her range. She's definitely taking a cue from the black
church and moving between pitches to set the mood. Stevie Wonder,
Donny Hathaway, and Prince all did a similar thing. They have entire songs that switch between vocal styles." The arrangement also
reminds us that Hill is marrying diasporas: an African American
deep soul tradition of hip hop weds the legacy of becoming a Marley. "She couples these black American gospel roots with a drum
roll that I associate with reggae. That drumming is kind of like a
marching band, but there's a one-drop element that's similar to dub,"
says Lynnée Denise. "She uses lots of space. That reggae bass line
lets you know she was listening to Sly and Robbie—and that she
was a good student. And of course, Carlos Santana's guitar is ridicu-
lous. I love that she forged this musical relationship with not just the
Marleys but Aretha, Carlos Santana, and CeCe Winans. She placed
herself in the conversation with legends, but she did it as a student
who learned so much from them it put her within the lineage of the
greats. Lauryn took the music seriously and continued traditions. I
love 'To Zion' for that. It's a pretty-ass song."

It was also a universally powerful moment of possibility, relatable for all women faced with pregnancy under unconventional

circumstances. For black women, however, it was a deeply needed affirmation—one we rarely get. "The decision to do motherhood on one's own terms is a kind of resistance," says Lynnée Denise. "And however black women decide to do it, is the 'right way.' Lauryn's response was to create a beautiful lullaby."

Tarana Burke "To Zion":

I was consumed with *The Miseducation* when it came out, and the song "To Zion" in particular. Remember, this was the reign of the cocky female emcee in hip hop, the era of Foxy Brown and Lil' Kim. They were all about storytelling, over-the-top extravagance, and sex. I mean, Lil' Kim was bragging about fucking and whatnot. That was cool and fun, but Lauryn was something in hip hop we hadn't seen. She was bringing a truth and a perspective to hip hop that I'd never heard before. She got at your heartstrings. Who writes about this? Who talks about this kind of black girl pain? That was reserved for girlfriends and journals. "To Zion" perfectly captured what I'd gone through in the early stages of my pregnancy and the deep, deep, deep feelings of love I was experiencing for my daughter, Kaia, this new human being.

Lauryn Hill, Erykah Badu, and I were all pregnant at the same time. I had just moved back to New York from Alabama, where

Kaia was conceived and born. While I was pregnant, I'd had a really terrible breakup with her dad, who was my high school sweetheart. I was struggling financially and emotionally. I was staying in the living room of my mom's house. I was at what I thought was the height of my career. It wasn't. It was really just the start of it. I was part of a group of youth activists across the country who were doing significant work and traveling around the country. I [had] just started to be recognized for my work in Africa and throughout the South. When I got pregnant, I can't say the response was exactly supportive.

I was twenty-three. I'd just graduated college, had a job, and was having a baby with the love of my life who, mind you, I'd been with since 1990. In my mind, I was grown, but everybody—my elders, peers, and family—was very much like "What are you doing? You're poised to accomplish this and that. Why would you have a baby right now? It's just going to slow you down." My mom definitely wasn't thrilled, which of course, she denies now. Even my movement folks were like, "This is not revolutionary. It's selfish." I felt like the most revolutionary work I could do was raise this little girl. We say that we're doing this movement work to create better communities for our people. How are we going to do that if we don't create examples of what the lives in those communities can look like? If I don't rise to the challenge of raising a child who is filled with love, kindness, compassion, respect, and one that has a critical consciousness, then I'm not doing my job in the beloved community. Don't tell me that it's not revolutionary to be pregnant. They were all so full of themselves, especially the men. Mind you, all of those Negroes are professors now and married with children.

Of course, now I can see that twenty-three is clearly still a baby, but back then, I was determined to prove everyone wrong. I was going to show them that my pregnancy wasn't going to stop anything. I went to Cuba with the Malcolm X Grassroots Collective when I was four months pregnant. The sponsors tried hard to stop me, and I was like, "I'm going." I went to the Million Women's March in Philly when I was eight and half months pregnant. I had to drive because my doctor wouldn't give me permission to fly. It was the dumbest thing I could have ever done but no one could tell me different. That continued even after Kaia was born. She was always with me, right by my side. To some degree, she's much better for it. It helped shape the person she's become. But I think I was also trying hard to prove to myself that my career wouldn't stop. I have to acknowledge now that it did. My peers from that time went on to do all types of stuff that . . . I just couldn't. At some point I made a decision that I wanted to be a certain kind of mother and that meant I had to say no to a lot of opportunities. I couldn't just pick up and go to Africa for three weeks anymore. Because when you're a mother you have to ask yourself those real questions like "Are you bugging? You've got a two-year-old at home." I credit my mom with being the voice of reason at that stage because she's the one who would say, "You've been gone for three weeks. Where is your daughter?" Me answering, "She's with the community. The community is taking care of her"? That wasn't going to cut it. I had to stop. So, I did, but I still clung to "To Zion." I would sing it to my daughter and change the words to "Beautiful, beautiful Kaia." "To Zion" was our little story. It resonated with me deeply. It still does.

This interview was conducted on October 7, 2017, the same day Harvey Weinstein's lawyer Lisa Bloom resigned, hoping to distance herself from Weinstein's mounting allegations of rape and sexual assault. On October 15, actress Alyssa Milano acknowledged Tarana Burke as the founder of the #MeToo movement and hashtag that has continued to galvanize women and demand accountability from industries across the country. On December 6, Time *magazine named Tarana Burke one of "The Silence Breakers" honored in 2017's Person of The Year issue.*

She did not stop.

I don't want to hear anyone say the word "defecate" anywhere near Nina Simone. Ever.

—dream hampton

4 / *We Told Her She Was Nina Simone*

The dénouement of the *Miseducation* moment seemed to start almost as rapidly as it began. By February 1999, New-Ark, the production team consisting of Vada Nobles, Rasheem (Kilo) Pugh, and twin brothers Johari and Tejumold Newton, filed a lawsuit in Newark federal court against Hill for allegedly failing to give them sufficient production credit and royalties for their work on *Miseducation*. In what they've since described as a "handshake deal" (otherwise known as the fastest travel route for friendships that want to arrive at a bitter end), they were paid $100,000 for publishing rights. After *Miseducation* blew the fuck up, they felt they were owed millions.

The "truth" of this is hard to determine but what is incontestable is that the accusation was definitely a blow to Hill's credibility. Much of the album's critical acclaim was rooted in the idea that she was a rare triple threat, but her collaborators were now claiming that they'd helped arrange all but one of the tracks on an album where she was credited as writer, producer, arranger, and sole executive producer. A year later, bassist Vere Isaac, who worked in sessions with Hill and Aretha Franklin on "A Rose is Still a Rose," filed a similar suit challenging Hill's claim that she was the Grammy-nominated hit's songwriter, claiming he'd written the melody.

In the case of New-Ark, the contention on both sides seemed to be a matter of degree. *Miseducation* did credit New-Ark with "additional production" several times on the album, as well as "additional musical contribution" and "additional lyrical contribution" on various songs, but the producers and their lawyer, Peter C. Harvey claimed their contributions were much more extensive and required a skill set far outside Hill's wheelhouse. "She is not a musician, she is not an artist," said Harvey to the *Los Angeles Times*. "[New-Ark] will make another album and everyone will see that they were the ones responsible for this album. I dare say that if you put Lauryn Hill in a studio alone, she couldn't do it again. Album number two for her is not going to sound like this." Two years later, the lawsuit was resolved in an undisclosed settlement from Hill, members of her management team, and record label. As for Harvey's speculation that a second album from New-Ark would prove their allegations, that never happened. The group never produced an album that rivaled *Miseducation*. Neither did Lauryn Hill.

dream hampton, one of the few critics that didn't like *Miseducation*, thinks Hill's claims were largely true because she considers the album's production its greatest flaw. "I love Lauryn, but I don't like that album," she says, noting "I Used to Love Him" and "Nothing Really Matters" are the only two tracks she enjoyed. "And I'm sure D'Angelo helped her produce 'Nothing Really Matters.' I actually like music, so I care about production," hampton continues. "Not that I wanted her locked in a relationship that was abusive, but she's under-produced. That's one of the things Wyclef did well for her, and it was missing on *Miseducation*."

Part of hampton's critique, she stresses, is steeped in the standard bearing legacy of black women who are singers, songwriters, and producers. "I'm nitpicking when I say I don't like it," says hampton, who compared Hill to Patrice Rushen in an early review. "I invoked Patrice Rushen because that's the level of mastery I think you needed. Production means more than tracks. Think about Puff producing Faith's background vocals for Mary's *My Life* album. Puff spent time with Faith—I'm talking two or three months, five and six hours a day, getting those background vocals. It was a production. He wanted Faith to sound like a whisper. He wanted it to sound like birds in a tree. I'm not saying it was the same thing as Cissy Houston singing background for Aretha, but it was some shit. There was real intention," she concludes. "When it came to production, I thought Lauryn was just playing around in the studio."

Reflecting back, hampton thinks that Hill's insistence on full credit may have been informed by the very gendered creative dynamics between Hill and her fellow Fugees. "Of course, this is me armchair diagnosing, but I think Lauryn was very insistent on having full credit because she'd been denied credit in the past. She was writing for the dudes in her group. She was writing Clef and Pras's lyrics and I don't think she always got credit for that. I think she wanted to appear in control—whether that was true or not. And I believe that to a large extent that it was because if Lauryn had real and experienced producers, someone like Kay Gee from Naughty by Nature or some other Jersey dudes, they would have talked her out of some of the poor choices she made. She didn't have anyone in the studio to pull her back from what I think are awful moments," hampton says, screeching an off-key bridge from "To Zion" to illustrate her point. "That was so bad. It stopped *Miseducation* from being a perfect album for me and it's not an album I listen to today."

In fairness to Hill, *Miseducation* was not her only writing and production effort. In addition to the contributions she made to Wyclef's solo debut *The Carnival* in 1997, for which she has producing and writing credits, she also wrote for CeCe Winans, Aretha Franklin, and Mary J. Blige with considerable success in 1999. However, whenever the extent of her musical capacities is discussed, the conversation gets reduced to the lawsuit. "People were challenging Lauryn's ability to produce and write her own lyrics; meanwhile she was out here producing three major giants," remarks Lynnée Denise.

"'A Rose is Still A Rose' was a great song both musically and symbolically because Aretha is known to be obsessive and difficult to work with—as she should be. She's earned that. Besides, we already know that when women know exactly what they want it's read as 'difficult,'" she says. "But what we also know is that Aretha Franklin is a supreme musician and therefore super specific about her production." And while the deejay concedes she wasn't impressed with the record's overall feel, she recognizes its importance. "It was a tad corny and a bit simplistic considering Aretha's long-standing relationship with complex composition, but I understood this duet to be the ultimate head nod toward Lauryn's ear and her evolving potential as a musician. What can't be denied," she concludes, "is that Lauryn made enough space for Aretha to feel at home in her runs. She gave those classic Aretha runs some hip-hop appeal."

Hill also continued her penchant for troubling musical genre binaries by blessing Winan's gospel track "On That Day" with a stone dub beat. The song was written while Hill was pregnant and is absolutely reflective of the late '90s moment broadly informed by a diasporic approach to black music and pregnant, like Hill, with possibilities. Lynnée Denise agrees, "'On that Day' is a solid, well-produced, and composed track that goes back to the work she did with the Fugees where she essentially Caribbeanizes these black American spaces. On this song Lauryn connected both [herself] and CeCe Winans to an accessible kind of global blackness. And she did it well. It was like *Sister Act* meets Kingston, or Black American church meets Kingston meets hip hop. That was a signature L-Boogie touch and straight out of her pages to add a reggae-inflected gospel track."

Connections and intersections. The point is underscored with the release of *Chant Down Babylon* in 1999. Produced by Bob Marley's son Stephen, the album features a mix of rappers—Guru, Rakim, yard bwoy Busta Rhymes, MC Lyte, The Roots, Chuck D (and the curious addition of lone rocker Steven Tyler)—all playing lyrical homage to the great Robert Nesta Marley. Its most touching moment is when Hill, mother-to-be to five of his grandchildren records a duet with a posthumous Bob on "Turn Your Lights Down Low." Given the spectator sport that was Hill's life just one year before, the moment is significant on multiple levels.

It confirms the identity of Hill's baby daddy, Rohan Marley, in a stunning music video that was partially shot from her newly declared address on Hope Road. Directed by *Hunger Games* trilogy director Francis Lawrence—who also shot music videos for Destiny's Child, Beyoncé, Jennifer Lopez, Will Smith, Lil' Kim, Janet Jackson, Justin Timberlake, and a few others, including fellow Fugees Wyclef Jean's "Gone til November" and Pras's "Ghetto Supastar"—the video is an odd moment of historical irony that mirrors Hill's leanings toward triangulated loves. Bob Marley wrote it for his lover, the 1976 Miss World, Cindy Breakspeare, the center of a celebrity love triangle—Bob, Cindy, and his wife, Rita Marley—that captivated spectators internationally. It was a complicated and, ultimately, well-negotiated cohabitation that lasted until the end of the elder Marley's life. Despite the sensationalism, history has also proven it a generative affair, resulting in two of Bob's most revered love songs—"Turn Your Lights Down Low" and "Waiting in Vain"—and their son Damian, an accomplished reggae musician in his own right and arguably the heir apparent. Similarly, Rohan Marley was also rumored to be married at the onset of his and Hill's courtship, however his marriage dates only really reveal that he wasn't divorced. The status of his relationship with his ex is unclear.

Hill and Rohan were never legally married during the course of their twelve-year relationship, but the video was clearly an attempt to marry their diasporic legacies, and it was full of visual signifiers selected to move seamlessly between past and present. It opens, for example, with a grainy sequence of then present-day Marley playing soccer, one that attempts to replicate vintage footage of his father playing soccer with the Wailers and company on Hope Road. The modest apartments where both Hill and Rohan each prepare for their date is another attempt, uniting their respective black histories with tchotchkes of both Marcus Garvey, the Jamaican ancestor of US black nationalism, and Bob, whose music served as a global ambassador to the vision of black liberation.

And while the visual of some woman jumping on the back of some fine-ass dred's bike is both common enough to hover around cliché and frequent enough to be hella real (it is certainly the point of my own son's origin) there is no question that both Rohan and Lauryn are just so stunning while doing it. Like fresh jelly coconut water, and sweet as chopped cane, Lawrence faultlessly captures the romantic dreamy beginnings of an on-island relationship. Slightly sticky, and slightly sweaty, it harkens back to the ephemeral point in love when everything is still beckoning and blurry and lacks all the peskiness of sharp focus and precise angles that inevitably develop with time and (five) kids.

Overall, the end result is a much more authentic use of place than the early Fugees videos for "Fu-Gee-La" and "Ready or Not," where Haiti was reduced to a nondescript backdrop for exotic, high-tech action capers. Here, Jamaica is front and center. Lauryn, by contrast, is seamlessly integrated into the culture as the video moves from recording sessions with the Marley brothers and the I-Threes to a bona fide reggae bashment—successfully bringing the latter to US hip-hop audiences a decade and change before Rihanna's "Man Down" in 2010 and "Work" in 2016. And since we're indulging in the game of hindsight, it seems worth it to note that Rihanna's versions—stylized, sensual, and sexier—are an easier read. Lauryn's, by comparison, is almost chaste. Even the dub with Rohan feels like the courtesy extended to a well-received and accepted visitor—a visa instead of citizenship.

Truth be told, *Chant Down Babylon* also served to massage an old wound. When Bob sang "play I on the R&B, I want all my people to see" on his song "Roots, Rock, Reggae" in 1976, it was a heartfelt plea to black American radio to give the Wailers airtime. Prior to his death in 1981, Marley struggled to connect with black American audiences, even agreeing to be the opening act for a 1979 tour with the Commodores—despite the fact that the Wailers were inarguably far bigger players on the world stage. Bob Marley died a few days shy of my fourteenth birthday. It was almost four decades ago, but I still clearly remember the shock of listening to New York's WBLS and hearing deejay Frankie Crocker play one of his songs in tribute. It was the first time I'd ever heard Marley played on black radio. As a first-generation Jamaican immigrant growing up in the Boogie, that moment to me is as clear and as significant as the first time I ever heard hip hop—"Rapper's Delight" to be exact—played on the radio. It marked the beginning of a substantial cultural shift and one that I could feel. Anti-immigrant sentiment was still real—it wasn't like people all of a sudden stopped telling us to get back on our banana boats. We were still coconuts, but I knew my teenage peers were now exposed to something that was culturally and politically so important to me. We could share it and talk about it.

So, *Chant Down Babylon* has a lot of resonance for me because it's literally the embrace Bob longed for by the children of the generation he failed to get it from. That the album's pinnacle love song is produced by his son Stephen and performed by the black American woman who was inarguably one of the biggest stars of the world—not just famous but like, *white* famous—was a moment that couldn't be ignored. This is not a universal sentiment. "C'mon," laughs Lynnée Denise. "MC Lyte is doing 'Jammin.'" I'm thinking about all those people who did covers on that album, and there's not one I want to hear more than I want to hear Bob. But I do think you're right about the video's Jamaica treatment." She pauses, then adds, "Honestly, I don't know what my thing is around Lauryn and her joining the Marley family, but I've been afraid to look at that."

I think about her hesitation and wonder if it has less to do with the Marleys than it does with that time period marking the untimely exit of accessible every girl L-Boogie for her more distant avatar, Ms. Hill. She made her appearance slowly, in a series of events that left fans with a palpable sense of loss.

In a July 21, 2001, live performance on the *MTV Unplugged* series, Hill opted to forgo her signature blend of hip hop, soul, reggae, and extensive live instrumentation and premiere twenty-two new songs accompanied only by an acoustic guitar and skills that were at best, nascent. Lyrically, the songs were a drastic departure from the universal themes explored in *Miseducation*. More aptly, they were strummed, esoteric sermons that critics found not only scattered and unfocused but deeply unsatisfying to audiences (and a label) who'd already been waiting three years for a *Miseducation* follow-up. The album *MTV Unplugged 2.0* was released the following year and sales were comparatively lackluster. It initially debuted at number three on the Billboard 200, but sales petered out at around 500,000. It's since gone platinum but back then it was widely considered both a commercial and critical failure.

It did have its fans. "You were one of the few people that like *Unplugged*," I say to hampton. She explains, "I'm more interested in it. I like the acoustic sound she was presenting and I saw an artist who was discovering herself. I think it's a more interesting album than *Miseducation*. There was a manifesto aspect to *Miseducation* that just wasn't interesting to me. Maybe it's because I was down with the hoes it was talking about. I'm down with the ones who were drug dealing, I'm down with the ones who were wearing weaves," she concludes. "Those are all my friends."

"What, Joan? Her *MTV Unplugged* performance? C'mon!" says Lynnée Denise when I tell her how I feel about the record. "The way she brought the guitar on stage randomly and all of a sudden? We'd never seen that from her before and she wasn't even afraid. She brought the guitar into conversation with her musicality and told us she was in the process of learning. And she shared that pro-

cess in a two-CD album with just her and her guitar." Yeah, Girl.
Not a fan. *Unplugged* was bold and bad. Still (hindsight, again), I
also think the album is weighted in discussions about Hill's legacy
in ways that are probably unfair. It was never meant to be evaluated
as the end of an oeuvre. The performance was meant to be a snap-
shot of Hill's creative and spiritual state. It was a moment. One that
got rewritten as an epic failure.

The lawsuit and *Unplugged* were followed up by a series of
high-profile events that caused Hill to languish in the court of public opinion. She was invited to the Vatican in 2003, where she delivered a scathing indictment of priests who commit child abuse, an
act that stunned some fans and alienated others. An over-promised
Fugee album and an accompanying reunion tour failed to manifest. Her highly anticipated follow-up record was ghost. Hill also
did herself no favors. In the summer of 2008, she kept more than
two thousand ticketholders waiting for almost three hours with no
more explanation than, "I have a problem with procrastination. I
have a great deal of difficulty deciding what to wear. It's a woman
thing." Lateness soon became a regular practice along with com-
plaints from fans and critics who found her performances increasingly erratic and unsatisfying. Hill, a former media darling, soon
earned a reputation as difficult, capricious, unreliable, and perhaps
most damning, insensitive to the time, pockets, and desires of the
fans who'd remained loyal throughout her career. In 2012, Hill was

convicted of tax evasion after failing to pay $1.8 million in federal taxes and she was sentenced to three months in jail.

Fans, fueled by a nostalgia for *Miseducation,* wanted the Lauryn Hill icon they'd fallen in love with. Instead they got an artist who would only perform reinterpretations of their favorites and often at speeds that made them unrecognizable. "I saw her at the Blue Note," Good Marable remembers. "We waited a couple of hours for her to get onstage. And then when she got there, it just felt like she really didn't want to be there. The way she performed the songs was so angry, almost frenetic. Just very chaotic, and so fast you could barely recognize the song. [If] I'm honest, there was a part of me that wondered if she was well," Good Marable confesses, recalling wigs, fashion choices, and makeup that seemed, to her, to border on bizarre. "Something happened. I don't know what it was. Maybe it was, 'I've got all these damn kids and people are on me wanting things from me all the time.' Lauryn gave a lot and I'm sure she wanted some respect," she concedes. "And I get that, but I also feel there was a lot of arrogance. Because no Lauryn, you aren't Nina Simone. And even Nina was not three hours late for a concert."

Hill, it seemed to some, had become undone and there were fans who looked for someone to blame. Tracing the trajectory of Hill's spiral, Solomon admits she was one of them. "It started with the second pregnancy. Then the release of 'Turn Your Lights Down Low,' which was followed by the complete scandal of *Unplugged*," says Solomon, who confesses she's still unable to watch it. "I was at the African Street Festival in Brooklyn the first time she arrived three hours late for a performance. She sang that lyric from *Unplugged*—the one about how she'd even thought about turning to women and everybody was like 'Oh my God, that Marley turned her into a lesbian!'" For the record, it was a big ol' leap. The lyric in question—from the song "Adam Lives in Theory"—talks about a symbolic Eve who is so disappointed with Adam's fuckboy-ness she considers bisexuality, but nothing in the song suggests that she's talking about herself. Still Solomon's recollections are hilarious. "Then there was the guitar playing. That wasn't good. There was something about it and her attempt at Rasta-ness that made me feel like her pull toward this culture was starting to make her a bad artist. Because before this she wouldn't have been onstage trying to pluck a guitar with Rohan peeking out from backstage. She would have gotten [music]—or stolen [it]—from decent guitarists."

As Solomon continues, her attempt at levity settles into something much more somber. "The idea that bad choices can affect what you produce as a woman has always really bothered me. Even though it's true, I don't like to admit it. I don't like the idea that if I'm fucking with somebody who's really fucked up that I'm going to make terrible things. It just seems like Lauryn's taste in men really affected who she was as an artist. The admission that even the great Lauryn could be reduced to making poor art and poor music and looking crazy and being late, over and over again, because of some random Marley . . . To me that felt like a betrayal."

"I think that Lauryn was mad at us," Good Marable offers by way of explanation, "But it was misdirected anger. I think she was really mad at herself and mad about her circumstances. I think she was pissed at the situation and she took it out on everybody else. I mean, 'call me Miss Hill'?"

I met Ms. Hill for an *Essence* magazine cover story I wrote in 2009. And yes, I did receive written instructions that she was only to be addressed as such. And yes, she did arrive late—which was typical of 99 percent of my experiences with rappers—but what was atypical was that she was late by weeks, not hours. Within minutes of her entering the room it was clear that Ms. Hill was not the Lauryn of *Miseducation*. This was a notably prickly and less cuddly incarnation, but what remained was also far too substantive to be written about with ridicule or as a has-been. I wrote this about our encounter: "When Ms. Hill finally emerges for the interview she is beautiful, petite, with an air that is palpably vulnerable, fragile even. Over the course of our hour-long conversation, one thing becomes exceedingly clear: Not only has L-Boogie left the building, but the Lauryn Hill icon we helped create may very well also have been an illusion. Her decision to become Ms. Hill liberates both herself and us from who we needed her to be."

And twenty years later, the truth that lingers is this: Ms. Hill refused to be what we wanted her to be and she was well within her rights to do so. We, however, were still years away from accepting her verdict. Or understanding that we were also at fault.

Think about it for a minute. Lauryn Hill was a twenty-three year-old *girl* who bared her soul and made a stellar, grown-ass-woman album. We were the ones who turned it into our bible. Then with gratitude and with ignorance, we did what we do with celebrities: We turn mortals into gods—queens, if they're only women—and then summarily pick them apart at the first hint of disappointment. So we told Hill she was royalty and crowned her the next Nina Simone. And then right after we thanked her for saving our souls, we summarily stripped away her humanity by demanding she do more. *Make another* Miseducation. *Come back Lauryn and save hip hop.* With five kids. Battling a lawsuit. As she was being carted off to jail for a conviction of tax evasion. And when she couldn't we began with the whispers. *Difficult. Jailbird. Side chick. You knew he was married right? No, not just him. The other one two. Crazy. Controlling. Demanding. Crazy. Crazy. Crazy.* I can only imagine that Hill must have also felt betrayed—by us. Perhaps twenty years later we can finally look at *Miseducation* and see where our culpability lies.

As black women, we really should have known better, but instead we did to Lauryn what the world does to us. Asks us to save it and when we do? It asks us to save it again. For present-day evidence look no further than the last presidential election, when 52 percent of white women voted for Trump and black women voted overwhelmingly for Hillary Clinton. Despite the fact that many of us were conflicted about her political centrism and corporate cronyism, we still showed up and did it like Yoncé, #InFormation. Why? Because black feminism has not only created and *gotten* intersectionality, we've done the work to make sure that black folks understand that every political possibility has to be measured by the variables of gender, race, and class to ensure an outcome that doesn't further endanger the lives of the marginalized. It's also a memo we've been sending to white feminists for years, and one that they've summarily ignored or forgotten to circulate. After the election results came in, what did white feminists so? Asked black women how to fix it.

Need more? It's common knowledge that Democrat Doug Jones owes us his 2017 victory over Republican pedophile Roy Moore largely because of the 96 percent of black women who not only turned up for him at the polls but organized other voters to make sure they did too. In a *Washington Post* article, Democratic National Committee Chairman Tom Perez broke it down like this: "Let me be clear: We won in Alabama and Virginia because black women led us to victory. Black women are the backbone of the Democratic Party, and we can't take that for granted. Period." And then what was the ask mere months after that? Oprah Winfrey made a beautiful, empowering, #TimesUp speech at the Golden Globes decrying sexual assault and white America responded by asking her to run for president. As if the 52 percent of white women who didn't vote for Clinton, a woman who, arguably, was one of the most experienced presidential candidates in US history *and* one who looked just like them, were going to suddenly vote for a black woman without white feminists once again, failing to do the critical work of intersectionality. *C'mon, y'all saved the world once. Can't you just do it again? And again?*

Didn't Zora Neale Hurston warn black women that we were the mules of the world? How wrong were we to jump on Hill's back and attempt to ride her? "I wish people would stop the public Lauryn yearning because if she has any anxiety, depression, stage fright, whatever it is, having people create this standard for her is not only going to not make her do anything different," reflects Solomon. "It's probably only going to make her feel bad. Also, I think people just got mean with it. *She needs to get it together. She's late all the time.* Because Lauryn seemed to have it so together. Because she was the It Girl, it looked like she's just fucking up, but I don't think that's what it is. I do know that Lauryn went to jail for owing money and people never talk about what the impact of that must have been. You're Lauryn Hill and you went to jail on some IRS shit. That is so traumatic. You had five kids and you had to go to jail? That is so embarrassing. Then you come out and have to deal with Wyclef and his stupid book? And people complaining about every show you do? I'm kind of like, 'Leave her alone.' Both the mean part and the 'Oh my God Lauryn, why won't you come back?' Maybe she just can't."

This is a struggle that Nadine Sutherland, who's been performing since she was a child, knows well. "I think that Lauryn is a sensitive artist who's misunderstood. I don't know if she felt burdened by all of those things that she was responsible for—creating a new narrative of African-ness for women in different places in the world, but I do know that we deify people and put them on this pedestal. The pressure of that is unbearable. And I know this because I've lived it." What about the lateness, Nads? Missed dates? "I'm not hearing this complaint. I'm not hearing any of that. Because in all these reviews people were giving Lauryn the middle finger. I am an artist," she continues. "And as an artist, what I see is an insecurity to face my crowd. I see the insecurity in having to wonder if they still like me. Do they still want me? Those are the struggles that I hear. As an artist who is struggling with all of that, I can definitely say that it hurts when somebody says something about me that's not true. It freakin' hurts. And I'm not even on the kind of world stage that Lauryn Hill was on." Sutherland concludes with the simple request that twenty years later we take some ownership. "We have to be honest about some of the stuff that was said about Lauryn Hill. It hasn't been kind. Even I look back and I'm like, I'm so sorry that I judged you, Lauryn. Because I did, when I saw her in Jamaica. I was like 'Girl!' I'm gonna be like singing, and she's gonna be singing along! But she didn't, and I couldn't and I was pissed because [I], the consumer, the Lauryn Hill fan, wanted her to act in the way that I expected.

"Lauryn Hill is a human being with human struggles. But when she walks into a room everybody wants her to make them feel as though they [are] still twenty years old. Everybody wants her to make them feel young and empowered. So they zone in on her instead of zoning in on themselves. Instead of zoning in on their relationship with God. That's a big responsibility, man. She is not here to make your life better. You are responsible [for making] your life better. So I don't think the emptiness [is] Lauryn Hill's. I think the emptiness is people who live in this world. Why do you need a savior? Why don't you save your damn ass self?"

"I remember thinking, 'I wish we could deal soberly with Lauryn,'" reflects hampton. "We should have been more sober about how we took her on, which should have been as a really good artist. In some ways, I look at Alicia Keys similarly. I remember Q-Tip saying, 'I wish Clive Davis would give her two or three more years.' Because if singing off-key has won you all these Grammies and all this attention, you're not going to stop at your ten-year point and say, 'You know what, I need vocal training.' Clive put her out too soon." hampton has a point. Elton John said something similar, and he was crucified for it. Keys has made some beautiful music, but she also made "Girl's on Fire."

"Or you get Lauryn Hill performing records at 140 beats per minute and manic," hampton continues. "How does this happen? It happened because we celebrated something that we considered the absence of something. She was the absence of the hoochie, the absence of the chickenhead, the absence of the rap ho. And we did that at the expense of looking at what was actually there, which was a solid egg that could have grown. What we did instead was crown her fucking Nina Simone. We did the same thing with D'Angelo. We told him he was Marvin Gaye and we told Lauryn that she was Nina Simone and they each had one fucking album. It wasn't fair to them because they started to believe it. But the Marvin Gaye we're talking about is the one that did a three-album suite that began with 'I Want You,' followed by 'What's Going On' and 'Let's Get It On.' They were really experimental, lovely, and meandering, but those three albums were made after a dozen albums with Motown. And Nina Simone did dozens of records, hundreds of records before we were like all 'Oh my God!' about 'Mississippi Goddam' or 'Little Girl Blue,' if you like the quieter stuff. There's this way that we crowned Lauryn. We really did. Look up articles.

You might have written it. I might have written it. But we invoked people like Nina Simone way too early and we conferred her with this legendary status that she had not earned yet."

This was as much a reflection of our shortsightedness as it was the time, claims hampton. "Certain eras, the '80s, the '90s through the early 2000s, have a different scale. It's not unlike trying to compare later films to those made in Hollywood's studio era. These later things had their own value, but we wanted something big. We wanted our own Madonna. We wanted our own big pop star. And Lil' Kim could've been that, but we just revert to our Christian shit so quickly. I'm sorry, what makes a ho again? Because Kim was fucking a married man? Well so was Lauryn. She was sleeping with someone's husband. Two someones' husbands because Rohan was married too."

hampton continues with a memory. "I remember once [the writer] Rob Marriott and I were walking in the Village and we saw this girl who was dressed kind of hoochie and she had a weave. Rob said, "If her hair was natural, it would be a totally different look." And it's like, Yeah man. If you look at Kim, Foxy, and Lauryn's outfits side by side, I bet Lauryn's shorts were a total of four to six inches. But she had locs, she was brown-skinned, and [she] did her makeup better. She wasn't trying to look like a Barbie doll. She was talking about fake hair and getting your nails done by Koreans—and I'm not even sure what's wrong with that—and we said, "Okay, that makes you good and makes these other women bad. And we need that right now because all this badness has killed our heroes and our icons. Lauryn Hill was messy, but she was exactly the kind of messy you're supposed to be in your twenties."

Say what you want about Erykah Badu, but Mama has always embraced her flaws. Rocked her messy like tribal scars. I often think about the kind of artist Hill could have become if she'd allowed herself to be free of our expectations, be beautifully messy and revel in her contradictions. Instead we put her up on a pedestal and then ordered her to remain there. And she did. Stuck. Much to her detriment and ours. hampton, however, reminds me that we had help. Hill, she says, was complicit. "I think that Lauryn thinks of herself as a prophet and I think we helped her to do that, and by 'we' I mean the public and the people who were writing about her. Because you're also alluding to the kind of protection we gave her and the ways we projected our desire for some kind of solution to what should have never been a problem. The bad girl isn't a problem. But there's always going to be that binary we create and project onto women who are just trying to live their lives."

Sometimes I think that Hill made such a strong commitment to upholding that version of herself that we almost had no choice but to hold her to it. I do wish she'd just given herself permission to just be, so that the next record didn't have to be birthed by a goddess. That to me is the core difference between *Miseducation* and *A Seat at the Table*. Whether or not we'll be talking about the latter twenty years from now, I have no way of telling. But I do know that the most liberating part of that album includes how humble and honest Solange is about her process. What we're seeing and what she's sharing, she reminded us at the 2017 Black Girls Rock awards, is a journey. One that is solidly rooted in *not* having all the answers and being tenderly public about it. That singular admission deads our mule shit and allows both Solange and her art to grow.

There's a critical part of *The Miseducation* we seem to forget. The album at its core was always about love, both the deciphering of it and the search for it. It's significant then, that during that opening snippet when the teacher, played by then-poet and now mayor of Newark Ras Baraka, reads Lauryn's name during roll call, she is the one student who is absent from class. Insistent and rebellious, she opted out of that protective environment and chose instead to learn those difficult lessons while being out in the world. "That's the reason I think *Miseducation* still holds up," says Jayson Jackson.

"A lot of people felt like Lauryn was telling us who she was on that record, but I'd argue that she was telling us who she wanted to be. You're hearing the hopes, dreams, and desires of a person both in a worldly and a spiritual sense. That's why we named it *The Miseducation.*"

Whatever the public's complex relationship may be to Ms. Hill, whatever the lingering, nostalgic lust for L-Boogie may be, it's important to underscore this: *The Miseducation* remains a revered, iconic piece of work. Twenty years after the fact. Good Marable has some thoughts about why. "*Miseducation* is a lot like *Thriller* to me. *Thriller* was not my favorite Michael Jackson [album]." Because *Off The Wall* is so much better. "So much better." She laughs. "But the thing that made *Thriller* amazing was the same thing that made *Miseducation* amazing. It turned a corner and shifted the culture. It was unlike anything that was happening at that moment. Lauryn made herself so vulnerable that it was super-empowering and that uplifted women. But Lauryn also disappeared, and I think there's a tendency to mythologize people who are gone too soon. We saw that with Biggie and Tupac. Lauryn was in her prime. It would be like Beyoncé disappearing after she had Blue Ivy. When you disappear, people tend to romanticize who you are and what you can do. Maybe she felt she had that Sade thing. That 'I'm going to drop an album and I'll see you in another ten years.'" But very few people can do what Sade does." Sade is bad as hell, I remind her, but even she didn't disappear until she'd dropped four consecutive albums and every single one of those was a banger.

I'm curious how Solomon feels, if she still plays the album. "I still play 'Nothing Really Matters' and 'Everything is Everything,'" she says. "And I'll definitely sing 'Ex-Factor' at any karaoke moment. That said, I don't play the entire album. I'm not going to play 'To Zion' for a range of reasons but mostly, I'm a childless, single black woman and that doesn't help me. But I'll put it to you this way, if the album comes on because I'm at whatever restaurant and they're playing the whole thing, I'm happy." She pauses for a moment, then confesses there is more. "When it comes time to choose music, I need it to put me in a certain mood. One thing that I didn't pick up on then that I can hear all through *Miseducation* now is that Lauryn was really depressed. Now I can listen to depressed singers—Donny Hathaway is my favorite singer of all time—and I don't know why Donny's okay, but Lauryn isn't. Maybe," she concludes, "Lauryn hits too close to home." Do you think it still holds up, Akiba? "Musically? Certainly. It is still 99 percent better than most of what I hear today. But as a piece of emotion, it takes [me] to a place that I don't really like to visit by choice."

I ask Good Marable what she thinks, ultimately. Was Lauryn Hill ever our Nina Simone? "We have to be careful of calling someone a legend. When you're as young as Lauryn was, that could be tough. We gave her all these accolades and I think they were deserved because the girl was bad. Make no mistake, the girl could write her ass off. She was bad as hell and we gave her her flowers. I think Lauryn does come from that same space of black genius as Nina Simone. But Nina had longevity and Lauryn did not." Solomon concurs, "I've heard people make comparisons to Nina Simone. I don't think it's all that, but I will say that nobody is touching what Lauryn did as a vocalist on that album. Not even Lauryn."

Mostly, however, what Solomon would like is for people to let the L-Boogie Lust go. "I'm not going to go see Lauryn in concert. I don't want to see her be really late and then sing songs in ways that nobody likes." But she also conceded that it's twenty years later, and that Lauryn might have been capable of things that Ms. Hill and her protective armor are not. "I would like another *Miseducation,* but Lauryn might not be capable of doing that. That happens to a lot of artists. It's an unfair burden. But I can leave it there because nothing in the world can unmake that one album. She gave it to us. That's her gift to the world." She leaves us with this bit of advice. "Just say thank you. And fucking keep it moving." She's right. We should. Because Lauryn Hill has done enough.

But there are other reasons to let go of the nostalgia. Holding on to L-Boogie while refusing to acknowledge the reality of Ms. Hill is a fatalistic surrender to the mistaken belief that black girl magic is an exhaustible entity, that the best isn't still yet to come. Twenty years later black female rappers are still breaking records. Cardi B's single "Bodak Yellow" marks the first time since 1998 that a solo female rap single has reached number one on the chart since Lauryn cleared that hurdle with "Doo Wop (That Thing)." There's been a lot of bellyaching in the comparative, the repeated complaint that Cardi's skills in no way measure up. Of course Hill is the superior emcee. That for me, however, isn't the point. Cardi is a girl from the Boogie who single-handedly turned herself from a stripper to one of the most recognizable artists in the world, on her own terms and with no fucks given to black respectability politics. There's a freedom in that, just as there is in the decision to love her "as is," in the way she chose to show up. Free, messy, and refusing to save the world.

My girl, journalist and filmmaker Raquel Cepeda, and I discuss our musing, thinking about what our ideal iGen raptress could be. For Cepeda it looks like this: "My dream raptress would be somebody that was the baby of [a] Lauryn Hill and a Cardi B. Somebody who can be, say whatever she wants to say. Including 'I don't give a shit motherfucker.' Who talks about sex any way she wants, but can also rhyme about the last book she read." Cepeda is hoping that the future will bring somebody "that's well-rounded. That doesn't have to tame herself. That can use social media in the successful ways Cardi B has. Own that she's a stripper but also have some introspection."

That, I agree, would be the 3.0. "The 3.0 and the artist that would make me bang down record label doors and try to become an A&R, because she's the missing one. That is it. The one that can say, 'Yeah, I've fucking held a gun. I have a temper. I'll fuck a bitch up. Whatever, but I want you to understand why I'm violent, and why I have anger issues. And I want to understand where we're at now . . . And that I like to fuck, and I like to read.'"

There are already hints of this, I think, as I listen to Cepeda. The Knowles sisters, for one. Solange in all the ways that we've already discussed but Beyoncé also. Because if you had told me twenty years ago when I was home writing the book on hip-hop feminism, back when most black women still considered it the other f-word, that one day there'd be a black female international pop star mastering global domination performing on stage with the word "feminist" towering mega-feet high behind her, I would have told you you were crazy. I also think of their actress counterparts, outspoken self-proclaimed feminists like Amandla Stenberg, Yara Shahidi, Zendaya, who are unapologetically crafting their feminist narratives and, in turn, creating new playbooks for us to follow. Lauryn Hill begat this. She paved the way for these girls. We all did.

5 / She Begat This: A Musical Guide to Remembering

I t seems right to end this how it began, bookended between a few rare nights out and in the company of my favorite millennials. Wynwood is not Harlem, but still the *Miseducation* is ubiquitous. Unlike most of the members in the canon of American classics, the kind we usually only play at home and fit neatly in the heart spaces relegated for nostalgia, nothing about *Miseducation* is dormant. No matter the night, no matter the venue, Lauryn Hill plays everywhere—whether the deejays are in their twenties or their forties. The album fills up real time and active space, shaping and informing human interactions.

This is a distinction I share with Douglas, who at twenty-six, finds this less surprising than I do. He remembers the first time he heard *Miseducation*. He was six years old, living in the Boogie, and he listened to it for the first time on his older cousin Maxine's Discman. Later, he remembers it always playing in her car and on the radio. Then, like now, it seemed to be everywhere.

"*Miseducation* was made twenty years ago, but I think, whether she knew it or not, she made that album for today." Intrigued, I ask him to explain. "Back then, it was a perception-shifting album, no doubt. But if you look at it now, and you look at what's going on in music, there is direct correlation. I think the things that she was trying to get across, the things that that group of individuals who collaborated on that album were trying to get across, still stand true today in a lot of ways—especially for millennials."

"Take a song like 'Superstar,'" he says, which he finds less judge-y than apt. The '90s he says, was the last real decade of live instrumentation in pop music. "There was no way we could have seen what was going to happen over time, the evolution of music, or how it would change. She was preaching about the music in her time and asking it to raise the vibration, but as millennials we can ask ourselves the same question today. Why are we stuck in the lower hertz level? Why is it not being used in a creative way to enhance consciousness or awareness?"

I think about this for a bit and decide to shift the convo's gears to love. Like the students who were in the album's skits and sharing their nascent reflections, Douglas was in elementary school. They're now in their late twenties to early thirties, veterans of love's game and intimate with its many contours.

The album dropped right at the brink of the digital age's explosion. Nobody was breaking up via text in 1999, I tell him. The observation makes him smile, so I continue with a confession. "I remember watching *Sex and the City* and being absolutely appalled when Berger broke up with Carrie via Post-it. That was like, a *thing* that very shortly after became routine. It seemed like everybody was carrying out their romantic affairs via email or text message."

Two thousand eighteen does love differently than 1998. Connections still meant telephone calls at least, if not a face-to-face conversation, I tell him. Then we laugh at the part in the "Everything Is Everything" video when old girl slams the receiver of the pay phone down, over and over and over again, clearly provoked by some fuckboy shit. "That existed," I said. "And if you were supposed to meet at the bridge in Central Park on the Upper East Side and you got stood up, your emotions didn't go immediately to pissed because anything could have happened. A delayed train, an accident, a string of broken payphones, the lack of a quarter. Now you can clarify all of that with a text."

"Yeah, I do think about that," he says. "Especially the fact that Lauryn was absent from the classroom and what she missed that day. The rest of the students got a place to think about love where they were protected by an unconditional love. I think she was absent because she was also fiercely independent. She needed to figure that out for herself, so she went to outside sources to get an alternate education." Hmmm. Love without the early safety net. I think about that and all the implications it has for a generation that is, from art to policy, reaping the '90s' gifts and its burdens.

"Our generation also had that alternate education. We had the Internet, the digital age, and Google. And because of it we seem much less able to connect." And he thinks, a little less patient than the generation before. "Because if you had to meet me in Central Park, on the Upper East Side at that bridge, there was no way for you to know if you got stood up, or if I missed the train, or if I had some kind of emergency until we talked or saw each other again."

So does *Miseducation* and its detailed chronicling of the heart still matter to them? He finds the question amusing. "I am sure there are plenty of millennials who grew up listening to *Miseducation* who couldn't wait to have their hearts broken so they could know what Lauryn was talking about. Our perception of love hasn't changed," he continues. "I think what's changed for us is its functionality in a culture of constant connectivity. I think 'love' for us is a way to disconnect from that constant connection. Love for us now, is the ability to sit in silence with someone." He elaborates, "No TV, no music, no phone, just super uncomfortable but comfortable silence. That for us, is love."

Note: This is different from "Netflix and chill."

Whatever one's opinion is of Lauryn Hill, let's close this out with the indisputable: As an early prototype of #BlackGirlMagic and an example of how to walk through the world as a black girl who rocks, we owe her. So I asked Beverly Bond, founder of Black Girls Rock and keeper of black girl legacies to close this out with a playlist honoring Lauryn's musical influences and the artists she paved the way for. Like Lauryn, Bev is a woman who also "begat" and she did it by challenging limited narratives about what a black woman could be, not by investing in binaries of good vs. bad but by offering up alternate examples of leadership, excellence, and most of all, black girl love. Because Bev's first language is music, and as a deejay she is legendary, I asked her to close us out with some love songs. Here's what L-Boogie begat:

The "She Begat This" Playlist by DJ Beverly Bond, Founder of Black Girls Rock, Inc.

"Everything is Everything" by Lauryn Hill

"Ex-Factor" by Lauryn Hill

"If I Ruled the World (Imagine That)" by Nas and Lauryn Hill

"The Score" by the Fugees

"Keep Ya Head Up" by Tupac

"The Sweetest Thing" by Lauryn Hill

"Sweet Thing" by Rufus and Chaka Khan

"Sweet Sticky Thing" by Ohio Players

"FEEL." by Kendrick Lamar

"untitled 03" by Kendrick Lamar

"Nothing Even Matters" by D'Angelo and Lauryn Hill

"Feel Like Makin' Love" by D'Angelo

"Zombie" by Fela Kuti

"Redemption Song" by Bob Marley

"Waiting in Vain" by Bob Marley

"Welcome to Jamrock" by Damian Marley

"Moonlight" by Jay-Z

"Weary" by Solange

"Didn't Cha Know" by Erykah Badu

"Womanifesto" by Jill Scott

"You Got Me" by The Roots featuring Jill Scott (Live)

"Heard 'Em Say" by Kanye West

"Champion" by Kanye West

"Four Five Seconds" by Rihanna (featuring Kanye West
      and Paul McCartney)

"Dear Mama" by Tupac

"My Life" by Mary J. Blige

"Have a Talk with God" by Stevie Wonder

"Black is the Color of My True Love's Hair" by Nina Simone

"Nobody" by Rapsody (featuring Anderson .Paak,
      Black Thought, and Moonchild)

"Be Free" by J. Cole

"Get By" by Talib Kweli

"Umi Says" by Mos Def

"Be Real Black for Me" by Donny Hathaway and Roberta Flack

"Pieces of a Man" by Gil Scott Heron

"Sponji Reggae" by Black Uhuru

"Just Like Water" by Lauryn Hill

"Spanish Harlem" by Aretha Franklin

"Masterpiece (Mona Lisa)" by Jazmine Sullivan

"Me and Your Mama" by Childish Gambino

"Rush Over" by Me'shell Ndegeocello and Marcus Miller

"Poetry Man" by Phoebe Snow

"Her Holy Water" by Imani Uzuri

"Love and Affection" by Joan Armatrading

"Fast Car" by Tracy Chapman

"Bad Habits" by Maxwell

Joan Morgan:

So, B Bond, is Lauryn Hill a #BlackGirlWhoRocks?

Beverly Bond:

Lauryn Hill absolutely rocks. And she rocks hard.

JM:

Tell us why.

BB:

When she speaks, she speaks truth. And she's uncompromising

about it in a way that's spiritual and speaks to our hearts. She dug deep to find her truth and then she shared it from a black girl's lens and from a black girl's experience. That was beautiful and unique. Lauryn Hill is an artist that walks in the most authentic version of herself, free from other people's expectations and burdens. And that's inspiring.

JM:

When we conceived "She Begat This," we talked about the playlist as a way to connect the dots between Lauryn Hill's musical contributions of the greats in black music that preceded her, those who she's clearly cut a path for and that she's inspired. Can you share why you thought this was important to do?

BB:

We live in a time that's so dismissive of legacy. It's an age where people are so quick [to dismiss] the greatness [of] those that came before them. There are new rappers now who say that Biggie and Tupac didn't matter and that's some dumb shit. That's really dangerous—especially for black people. When we erase our origins, we risk losing our culture and we leave it vulnerable to other people who want to just pick it up and run away with it. So, I get it when some journalist writes an article about why we need to give up on Lauryn Hill, and someone like Talib Kweli responds with an article about why white people need to stop telling black people who we need to give up on. We can't get caught up in other people's dismissals because our circumstances aren't the same. Lauryn Hill is a successful black woman, but she's also one that's lived a black girl's experience. Given the things that all women go through and black women in particular, that means she's had some trauma in her life. None of that erases her greatness—in the same way that Gil Scott Heron's struggles [with addiction] didn't erase his.

JM:

What would you say to the critics who'd argue that *The Miseducation of Lauryn Hill* was a singular success and that great musical legacies are created on a body of work and multiple successes?

BB:

I'd say she is great. And not only is she great, she gets better and better at it. I can't say this enough: Lauryn Hill is an artist who does what she wants to do. She chooses whether or not to share her work with the world or keep it to herself. That kind of respect for her own genius is something we all need to appreciate. And she has more work than just *Miseducation*. The new stuff that's coming is even iller than before. When she puts it out, it's going to be amazing. I think people who say "Lauryn's lost it" or wonder if she's ever going to come back haven't seen her perform. She's been back.

JM:

Can you give an example?

BB:

Sure. In 2015, I curated a hip-hop festival at the Kennedy Center called Rock Like a Girl. I asked Lauryn to be the headliner, and she agreed. She killed it. Because of her the show sold out. There were lines around the corner, standing room only, and it was magnificent. Nas performed the same festival the night before, and he also sold out but believe me when I tell you that the crowd for Lauryn wasn't just huge, it was so much bigger. There were people waiting around just in case people would come out. And I tell you, as soon as she got on the stage, there wasn't a person in their seats. Maybe there was a time when she did have moments on stage that weren't so stellar. So, she's been late. She's not the only artist that's been late. Artists are always late. There's this anti-Lauryn energy in the world that I don't understand, but what I really don't understand is when we as black people participate in it—especially black women. We have to hold our sister tight, hug her, and elevate her. We can't be the ones on social media dissing her. People do less criticism of R. Kelly than they do of Lauryn Hill. Sometimes I feel

like there's an attack on Lauryn that's basically because her truth—
her power to the people and to blackness—is so deep.

Rock Like a Girl showed me something about Lauryn Hill.
She came through for that festival because she'd been paying close
attention to Black Girls Rock. I know this because I was told in
no uncertain terms, "Bev, she's doing this for you." Now Lauryn
doesn't really know me, but she feels that the work that I'm doing
for black women and girls is important. Her statement about being
on the show was, "I am here for black girls." She's here for us.

JM:

And really always has been.

BB:

Always has been. Which is why we have to be there. Lauryn Hill
was great, and she loved and worshipped black people. You have
to appreciate when that happened in your lifetime and in your
generation. You have to appreciate her the way you appreciated
Stevie Wonder or the way you appreciated Nina Simone. Lauryn
Hill nurtured a rare, beautiful genius until it became her
superpower. That will always matter.

JM:

So, let's talk about these songs.

BB:

The Lauryn Hill songs I chose for this playlist—"Everything is Everything," "Ex-Factor," "Just Like Water"—are some of my favorites. I chose "The Score" because I wanted some Fugee representation, since it's her point of origin and because her work on that record is amazing. I chose "The Sweetest Thing" because it represents the sensual side of Lauryn. That was one of the things she brought to her music. It wasn't all spirituality and community. It was sensuality as well and the combination reflects how well-rounded she was. I love that.

JM:

I love that you included Chaka Khan's "Sweet Thing" and Ohio Players' "Sweet Sticky Thing" in your collection of "sweets." Phoebe Snow, Roberta Flack, Aretha Franklin. They all really speak to that sound, the archive of soul greats that she's so clearly inspired by and whose DNA is all over *Miseducation*.

BB:

When I thought about Lauryn and Chaka, I thought [not only] about Chaka's voice, but the energy and depth of her artistry as well. You know, a lot of people miss that because they just focus on her sensuality but there's so much more to her. There's also a link between Chaka's faith and her art, that's similar to Lauryn. Chaka is the complete package, so to speak. And Lauryn is very reminiscent of Chaka in that way.

JM:

I feel she influenced their later work too. There's that great moment when she writes and produces Aretha Franklin's "A Rose Is Still a Rose" and it goes up against "Doo Wop (That Thing)" for Best R&B Song of the Year which means Lauryn was essentially competing against herself. No way, you know I'm going to go look for you now. Let's talk about Tupac. I think that there are some people who might be surprised to see him on here, but if you think about it, they're artists who shared some of the same trajectory. They've both had incredible highs in terms of artistic achievement and they've both known the lows of a prison sentence. In some respects, both Tupac and Lauryn were trapped by the limits of public personas that masked their complexities.

BB:

I feel like Tupac and Lauryn are kindred spirits. He and Lauryn are cut from the same cloth in a lot of ways. Both of them utilized their art as a kind of activism and healing for black people. Their love for community was real and with Tupac, you can really see that in a song like "Dear Mama."

Kanye?

I love Kanye! You know when we think of male rappers we tend to think that their only musical influences are other men and I just don't think that's true—whether they admit to it or not. I think they were also influenced by some of the women and Lauryn is certainly one of them. When Kanye does that introspective lesson/sermon thing on "Heard 'Em Say," I can hear Lauryn's influence on him because that's something that she mastered. So, if he's going to go down that lane, I'm gonna have to give Lauryn Hill some credit for it. Kanye also produced Talib's "Get By." Talib and Lauryn are very close and when you listen to the composition of that song, you can hear the ways they were influencing each other. Same goes for Mos Def. Lauryn was an artist he could turn to for inspiration, depth, and truth. Childish Gambino, J. Cole, and Kendrick Lamar are on here for similar reasons. And both Drake's "Nice for What?" and Cardi B's "Be Careful" sample tracks from *Miseducation*. Sometimes when we talk about great people in hip hop, Lauryn doesn't get the credit she deserves because people feel that she doesn't have enough work. Yet the work she does have showcased these levels of depth and complexity. Kendrick is an artist who exhibits the same kind of depth and layered complexity that Lauryn Hill absolutely represents. So, when I think about Kendrick's influences, I definitely have to add Lauryn Hill to that list. When I look at these young artists like J. Cole and I think of their influences, I'm going to consider Lauryn. Because when you hear "Be Free" you can't really point to Biggie or Jay. You'd have to point to a Nas, a Mos Def, or a Lauryn. Same for Rapsody. I love that she's new and different. She's trying to go deeper and trying to take us back to the hip hop that was lyrical, stylized, had cadence and flow and content that mattered. She's definitely walking in that Lauryn Hill space. I don't think they give her enough credit and she still managed to get nominated for that Grammy with all them dudes.

JM:

D'Angelo being on here feels so right to me and not just because he and Lauryn collaborated on "Nothing Even Matters" for *Miseducation*. They're both artists who resisted market demands and public pressure to put out albums before they were ready to do it. And they got a lot of criticism for it. But they both took time also, lived their lives, and went through their challenges. Ultimately, I think the work is better for it. Same goes for Maxwell.

BB:

When it comes to their artistry and the way they approach it, I
think those three are all kindred spirits. They're all influenced
by the fullness of the musical legacies that came before them
and it gives their work layers and dimension. First and foremost,
they do their art for themselves and they do it when they want
to. We forget that we can't command great artists to create for
us on demand, and when they do we usually get something
that's different [from] what we love that artist for. Maybe some
people can do it, and it's okay if they can. If you make pop
music especially, then that ability is great. But when I know that
if [we] wait on an artist's authentic process that we're going to
get some level of greatness, I'm not going to put a rush on him.
I'm going to wait. And if Stevie Wonder wants to make one
album every ten years, I'm gonna go buy that album because
Stevie made it.

JM:

There's such a parallel between Stevie's "Have a Talk with God"
and Lauryn's "Tell Him."

BB:

It's that beautiful moment that you turn to when life is hard,
and you decide to just go have a talk with God. It's not about

the religion that he chose to sing it through. It's really about him telling you that in order to get through it you're going to have to go within and speak to the Spirit. Speak to the light force. Speak to the universe, meditate, and then take those moments to determine your truth. Lauryn also does that for us on "Tell Him." I definitely think she's been influenced by Stevie Wonder.

JM:

The playlist includes so many of the genres that Lauryn references in her work—soul, hip hop, reggae, R&B—but it also takes a diasporic approach to black music. I mean Fela Kuti is on here.

BB:

Lauryn's rhythms are definitely influenced by reggae, Bob Marley being the most obvious, and not just because she's now a member of the Marley family. I chose Black Uhuru because they have that soulful reggae sound with a strong beat and bass that always felt like just the right amount of sexiness. It feels like that moment when you first walk into the room and you know the mood and the vibe is right. That cool that's just part of the black experience. It felt like the kind of party Lauryn would have been at. As far as Fela Kuti, Lauryn uses a lot of African music. She did a remix

of "Lost Ones" with "Zombie" at Rock Like a Girl and
when I tell you she murdered it, it was so beautiful, Joan.
She started with "Lost Ones," mixed in "Zombie," then she
brought out the African dancers. It was so dope. Fela's art
was so grounded in resistance and his truth—that raw truth
that people are scared of, you know? Again, very similar to
Lauryn. She also performed this song called the "The Meek
Shall Inherit the Earth" that she's never released. When we
were editing the show every single one of the editors—all
of them young white guys—played that back over and over.
Everybody listened to that song, young and old, black and
white, and people were really rooting for her. It was like she
touched everybody's spirit all over again, just like 1998
or 1999.

JM:

The playlist made me remember how many collaborations
Lauryn's done with other artists—female and male: Jill Scott,
Mary J. Blige, Nas, The Roots.

BB:

Yeah. Lauryn is an artist that is able to cocreate. It's given us some
beautiful stuff. I have Nas and The Roots on here because I like
that combination of energy between men and women singing

together and creating together. It reminded me of Lauryn's days in the Fugees. Or Roberta Flack and Donny Hathaway. The blackness and the realness, the duets.

JM:

I think Mary J. Blige's *My Life* has got to be one of my favorite '90s black-girl moments ever. That album and *Miseducation* didn't just provide us with soundtracks for our lives, they give us the catharsis we needed.

BB:

They were both so raw and vulnerable. Their gift to us was that they were able to remain so unguarded in their art. They let their pain out for us to see and that gave us permission to release our own. Mary literally sang our pain, you know. So did Lauryn.

JM:

There've been a lot of comparisons made between Solange's album *A Seat at the Table* and *Miseducation*. Why did you include her on the playlist?

BB:

Solange has been making some really good music for a long time, but *A Seat at the Table* is one that's very reminiscent of

Lauryn Hill. It's an album about that inward journey and it's delivered to us in sermons that make us also turn inward. Great music does that. You can just tell that Lauryn is one of Solange's influences. Both Solange's "Weary" and Erykah Badu's "Didn't Cha Know" offer up layers of their hearts. They're both very introspective songs that offer lessons through these musical sermons. Lauryn was one of the rare artists [who] was able to do that without finger-pointing. Erykah and Solange do that here too.

JM:

Yeah. I definitely feel that Lauryn offered Solange a template for what a black woman's vulnerability and exploration could look like. Lauryn didn't have a template from her generation. She had to find that in the previous generations' soul singers. But as for how a woman could do that with hip hop and R&B, she had to create that model for herself. People sometimes forget how hard it is to be the first.

BB:

And I absolutely see that as a problem. It also speaks to how great Lauryn really is because she had to pioneer the territory, and that's no easy road. That's how you get something like

Jazmine Sullivan's "Masterpiece" [in] that she talks about being comfortable with who you are because you're already born a masterpiece. The power in Jazmine's voice, its rawness and its soulfulness remind me of Lauryn. That's why Rihanna's on here. She's certainly pop, but she has a rawness, [an] edginess that comes from walking your own path. I feel Rihanna can do that because that ground has already been broken. Lauryn paved the way for that freedom and Rihanna inherited it. And I think that's beautiful.

JM:

And that freedom to just be herself was hard-earned. We owe her for that.

BB:

Because what happens if we don't have that music to inspire us? I had to call somebody out on it one time because she was arguing that Lauryn didn't matter because she hasn't done anything lately. Why do you think that's okay to publicly slam somebody for no real reason? Or make them a joke, especially someone who's given us such greatness. Because where would we be without her? Jay-Z's "Moonlight" is on here because he reminds [us] of what they

did to Lauryn Hill. They sent this woman to jail. We can't
be the ones to critique this woman [without] acknowledging
what happened to her. This black woman has represented us
in such a huge way. So stop. Please stop.

JM:

I think people also forget what the climate was like when
Miseducation came out. While writing this book I had to go
back and look at how we were being represented in the late
'90s. It was a really hard time to be a woman in hip hop,
or one who loved hip hop. We needed Lauryn so badly. We
needed the win.

BB:

We did. Yeah, we did. We absolutely did.

JM:

She gave it to us and then people turned right back around and
burdened her with saving the genre. For years it was like, "Come
back and save hip hop." With five kids. I have a hard enough time
working with one. I was like, "Hasn't she done enough?"

BB:

Exactly. Why are we demanding that of this woman?

JM:

Especially black women. Because it's not like we don't know that we're always being asked to save the world.

So, let's finish this out with Nina Simone.

BB:

Why Nina Simone? I mean, that's just obvious. Lauryn Hill is our generation's Nina Simone. She's our Nina. That's who she is.

Acknowledgments

Maferefun gbogbo Egun, especially Miss Ann, Celia, Victor, Merriam, Grandma Rachel, Tall Walking Joe, Organza, Bird, and The Koramantee. To answer your question, Bird: "Yes. I have met me. Finally." *Maferefun Elegba*, for the doors you opened and the ones you closed and for the words of guiding wisdom from your son Esu Adewa. *Maferefun* to my mother Yemoja and my "Auntie" Oshun for taking the wheel. *Maferefun Olokun* for teaching me to pay less attention to how much farther there is to swim and more to the fact that I have never drowned.

To my agent Sarah Lazin and my editor Rakesh Satyal, thank you for the opportunity to tell this story and the unerring faith that I could, even in the face of harrowing deadlines. To the ATRIA crew: Yona Deshomme, Loan Le, and Stephanie Mendoza, how many thanks? Many, many. Mi seh many many many.

To my chair Dr. Jennifer L. Morgan, to whom I owe a significant debt (not to mention a dissertation) for not freaking out when

I walked into her office and told her I need a few months off to write a book, thank you. Nuff love to Young Arts LA 2018 staff, writing finalists, and my co-directors Roger Bonair-Agard and Ron McCurdy for equal parts support, gracious tolerance, and inspiration. Rebekah Lengel, your chill was my calm. I'm grateful for that.

All books are born, and some births are more difficult than others. This one had some of the best midwives a writer could imagine. Akissi Britton, Daniel José Older, and Patrice Fenton, there simply aren't enough words to express the depths of my love, respect, and appreciation for the ways you've held me down. I have to trust that you already know. Similar sentiments go to my fellow fly girl from The Boogie: Lisa Leone for prayers, the guest house, yoga, laughter, good wine, food, and even better coffee. Seriously Mama, who's better than you? And really, who's better than Jimmy? Elizabeth Sobol, thank you for the gift of shelter and the sea. To the Jacobs family: Gizelle, Schott, Nika, and Schottie, for a home away from home. And sushi. Did I mention sushi? Mitzi Miller, thanks for bringing up the rear in the ways only you can, with equal parts drama, hilarity, efficacy, and shopping. My family is an amazing bunch. Mom, thank you for giving me the space to do the work and keeping me in constant prayer. Eternal gratitude to my brother, Gregory Morgan, and sister-in-law, Angel Howard, for everything from receiving panicked phone calls to expediting forgotten notes across country and loving texts to cheer me across the finish line.

When it comes to hip hop, the contributions of women writers and cultural critics are too often treated as afterthoughts, the lone voice meant to give "the female perspective" in a discourse people still assume belongs primarily to men. I'm incredibly grateful to the writers, deejays, scholars, critics, and artists—the former 90's fly girls whose rich contributions to this book prove we were not only there but integral to the very foundations of perhaps the most significant cultural movement of the late 20th and early 21st century: Belinda Becker, Yaba Blay, Beverly Bond, Tarana Burke, Raquel Cepeda, Michaela Angela Davis, Lynnée Denise, Joicelyn Dingle, dream hampton, Treva B. Lindsey, Karen Good Marable, Akiba Solomon, and Nadine Sutherland. Kierna Mayo, your foreword to this book set "the bar" for the bars. Thank you for making it all the things. Jayson Jackson, Schott Free Jacobs, and Robert Kenner, this would have been a very different, and frankly, incomplete book without your memories and insights. Thank you, Brethren, thank you. Douglas Galluzzo, you started out as an interview subject and ended up Fam. Your gifts are too many to mention.

Special shout-outs to Jeff Chang, Brittney Cooper, Zahara Duncan, Marc Lamont Hill, Mark Anthony Neal, and Brittany Williams. Fam is fam is fam is fam.

Finally, my greatest gratitude goes to the absolute creative genius of Ms. Lauryn Hill, without which none of this would have ever been possible.

About the Author

A pioneering hip-hop journalist and award-winning feminist author, Joan Morgan coined the term "hip-hop feminism" in 1999 with the publication of *When Chickenheads Come Home to Roost*, which is now used at colleges and universities across the country. Joan has taught at Duke University, Stanford University, and The New School. She is currently a doctoral candidate in American Studies at NYU.